T0287937

JOHN H. BURDAKIN
AND THE GRAND TRUNK
WESTERN RAILROAD

John Burdakin (*right*) shows off a Grand Trunk Western locomotive in the shadow of Detroit's Renaissance complex in 1977. Looking on are International-Stanley's Ed Kelling (*left*) and Jim DiBona (*center*). (Photo courtesy of Michigan State Railroad Museum)

JOHN H. BURDAKIN AND THE GRAND TRUNK WESTERN RAILROAD

Mary Sharp and Frederick J. Beier

Michigan State University Press

East Lansing

∞ The paper used in this publication meets the minimum requirements of ANSI/NISO
Z39.48-1992 (R 1997) (Permanence of Paper).

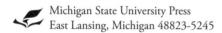 Michigan State University Press
East Lansing, Michigan 48823-5245

Printed and bound in the United States of America.

26 25 24 23 22 21 20 19 18 17   1 2 3 4 5 6 7 8 9 10

LIBRARY OF CONGRESS CATALOGING-IN-PUBLICATION DATA

Names: Sharp, Mary. | Beier, Frederick.
    Title: John H. Burdakin and the Grand Trunk Western Railroad / Mary Sharp and
Frederick J. Beier.
    Description: East Lansing : Michigan State University Press, 2016. | Includes
bibliographical references and index.
    Identifiers: LCCN 2016000401| ISBN 9781611862218 (cloth : alkaline paper) | ISBN
9781609175061 (PDF) | ISBN 9781628952797 (ePub) | ISBN 9781628962796 (Kindle)
    Subjects: LCSH: Burdakin, John H. (John Howard), 1922- | Burdakin, John H. (John
Howard), 1922—Philosophy. | Grand Trunk Western Railroad Company—History. |
Grand Trunk Corporation—History. | Executives—United States—Biography. | Grand
Trunk Western Railroad Company—Management—History. | Grand Trunk
Corporation—Management—History. | Management——United States—Philosophy.
    Classification: LCC TF25.G68 S53 2016 | DDC 385.092—dc23 LC record available at
http://lccn.loc.gov/2016000401

Book design by Scribe Inc. (www.scribenet.com)
Cover design by Erin Kirk New.
Cover photo of John H. Burdakin is used courtesy of the Michigan Department of
Transportation Photo/Video Unit.

g green Michigan State University Press is a member of the Green Press Initiative and
  press is committed to developing and encouraging ecologically responsible
INITIATIVE
publishing practices. For more information about the Green Press Initiative and the use of
recycled paper in book publishing, please visit www.greenpressinitiative.org.

Visit Michigan State University Press at www.msupress.org

This book is dedicated to the people, like John H. Burdakin, who have learned how to be successful in business while also having a successful and fulfilling home life. It is the balance we all seek and that this book supports.

Contents

A Thanks from John H. Burdakin   ix

Foreword by Dennis J. Gilstad   xi

Introduction   xv

Important Dates in the Life of John H. Burdakin   xxiii

Chapter 1. When Put in Charge, Take Charge   1

Chapter 2. Do the Right Thing   19

Chapter 3. When You See a Problem, Find Solutions   29

Chapter 4. You Won't Win Them All   41

Chapter 5. Hire Good People   49

Chapter 6. Choose Carefully Whom You Marry   55

Chapter 7. Enjoy Your Work and Work Hard   59

Appendix 1. An Overview of Grand Trunk   67

Appendix 2. Shared Values by the Burdakin Family   81

Appendix 3. Jean Burdakin Essays   89

Appendix 4. This I Believe   95

Notes   101

Index   107

This photograph shows the engraved bronze plaque presented to John Burdakin in 1987 upon his retirement from the Grand Trunk Western Railroad. Artist Stephen McVeigh created the plaque, which recounts the professional and personal highlights of Burdakin's life. (Photo from John H. Burdakin collection)

A Thanks from John H. Burdakin

WHEN I WAS FIRST APPROACHED ABOUT A BOOK ON MY CAREER, I WAS overwhelmed and found the offer hard to believe.

I hope we have material in this book that people will find useful. It would make me proud if someone finds something worthwhile in reading about my approach to life and to work.

Over the years, I've seen my name in print frequently. But I never thought of my life, when I was working Monday through Saturday, as any kind of model for others. I am extremely honored that Dennis J. Gilstad thought my achievements worthy of a book.

I've enjoyed my life, my family, and my work. There are a lot of things I didn't get done and won't get done in my life. But I did get many more things done than I ever anticipated when I was growing up in Wollaston, Massachusetts, during the Great Depression. I know that many people didn't have the opportunities that I did. I am humbled by the support I received during my career from many admirable individuals. For their efforts and friendship, I am most appreciative.

It does seem it's the time in my life to tip my hat and dance off the stage. The spotlight is dimming, but I take my final bow with a deep sense of gratitude and thanks.

John H. Burdakin

Foreword

DENNIS J. GILSTAD

JOHN H. BURDAKIN IS THE BEST RAILROAD MANAGER I'VE HAD THE pleasure to know, and I've known a great number of them.

I believe it will be helpful for students in the railroad management school I founded at Michigan State University to read about the principles that guided John during his years with the Pennsylvania Railroad/Penn Central and then as head of the Grand Trunk Western Railroad. These principles, in fact, will be of interest to anyone who aspires to be an effective manager, of a railroad or otherwise, and to have a fulfilling personal life.

John Burdakin was one of the first professional managers in the railroad industry, and his example and leadership helped humanize a rough-edged business. John was clear and calm at a time when many of his peers were brash and belligerent. He emphasized communication. He listened. He was decisive and goal-oriented. He treated everyone with respect—at least until they failed to show him respect in turn.

John told me he wishes he'd made an effort to keep me at Grand Trunk Western when I resigned to start my own business, that he wishes he'd asked me what department I wanted to run and then made it happen. But, we agreed, my success with my own companies worked out well for me and, I hope, for future railroad managers.

John believed in continuing education for the managers who worked for him, sending executives to professional conferences and to three-month management courses at Harvard. But he told me, after he'd visited the railroad management school at Michigan State, that he wishes he'd invested even more in training.

That's the point of this book and of Michigan State's railroad management school—to educate the industry's current and future managers.

It's important to note that as successful as John was at running railroads, he had an equally successful home life with his wife, Jean, and their three sons, John Jr., David, and Dan. The family moved many times in the course of John's career. Jean, whose motto was "Bloom where you're planted," was the family's calm, capable center. You'll hear from the Burdakin family in this book, too.

In my years of working with John, and then being his friend, I saw that John's professional goals extended beyond running a business that made money, though he certainly understood both sides of a ledger. The end goal in business—he believes, and I believe—is to benefit the community. Managers must focus on their relationships with people. If they do that—he believes, and I believe—the profits will come along.

With John's help, we identified Ten Principles of Management that guided his career and home life. The principles, which are discussed in this book, are:

- Safety first.
- As a motto: Always do the right thing.
- When put in charge, take charge. Look like a boss, talk like a boss, act like a boss. Stand up and say clearly what you want and expect.
- Don't worry about what people say. If you're the boss, you are, at some point, going to be thought of as a "spherical SOB," whatever you do.
- When you see a problem, find solutions, and do not back away until a solution is found and implemented.

- Realize from the outset that you won't win them all.
- Hire good people, then leave them alone to do their jobs—but make sure they keep you informed.
- Choose carefully whom you marry. Ninety percent of your happiness or unhappiness depends on this decision.
- Enjoy your work—and work hard to achieve your goals.
- Be honest. Live a life of integrity.

John Burdakin died in his sleep on September 11, 2014. He was ninety-two and was singing to his caregivers the night of September 10 right before he went to sleep. He exited this world with as much class as he inhabited it.

I miss John and the thoughtful discussions we had over the years. I valued his friendship and his hard work on this book. He completed his final meeting on this manuscript three days before he died, and he was so humble—and so gratified—to know there would be a book devoted to his management principles.

I wish to thank my longtime friend Gary M. Andrew for his remarkable management of this book, with thanks also to the Burdakin family, Frederick J. Beier, William Litfin Sr., Ann Noble, Mary Sharp, Howard M. Tischler, and the Michigan Railroad History Museum in Durand, Michigan.

I also must mention the contribution of Edward A. Burkhardt, another excellent railroad manager whose influence and railroad holdings span the globe. His generous gift made the railway management school at Michigan State possible. I am forever in his debt, as are the current and future students of the school. Thank you, Ed.

Chicago mayor Richard Daley uses a simulated railroad switch-key to open Grand Trunk Western's new intermodal terminal in Chicago. On hand for the ceremony were John Burdakin (*left*), president of Grand Trunk Western, and his boss, Robert Bandeen (*center*), president and CEO of Canadian National. (Photo courtesy of Michigan Railroad History Museum)

John Burdakin talks with President Gerald Ford during a visit to the Grand Trunk Western Railroad in 1976. (Photo courtesy of Art Fettig)

Introduction

MUCH OF THE SOURCE MATERIAL FOR THIS BOOK COMES FROM PER-
sonal interviews with John H. Burdakin in the two years before his death in
September 2014.[1] We have attempted to provide clear attribution to facts,
opinions, and statements. In addition, we have provided explanatory notes for
terminology or concepts that may be unique to the railroad industry as well
as putting a chronological orientation in each chapter to the experiences of
Mr. Burdakin. We have taken the liberty of combining some of Burdakin's ten
management principles, as outlined by Dennis J. Gilstad in the foreword, in the
chapters that follow, and we have summarized each chapter with a list of "Takeaways." As such, this is not a traditional, chronological biography.

John Burdakin started his railroad career and learned his craft at the
Pennsylvania Railroad (PRR) in 1947. He experienced the merger of the PRR
and the New York Central Railroad (NYC) into the Penn Central, as well
as its demise. He migrated to the Grand Trunk Western Railroad (GTW)
in 1971, where he was president from 1974 until 1986. It's important to
understand the magnitude of change that occurred in the railroad industry
over that period of time. For example, railroads emerged from post-World
War II recovery to financial hardship under regulation, then de-regulation
and severe intermodal competition. As you read about the career of John
Burdakin, some context is useful to put his story into perspective.

THE LEGACY OF REGULATION

Railroads were the first major corporations to be regulated by the federal government—starting with the Interstate Commerce Act of 1887.[2] The focus of regulation was to protect the interests of the shipping public by providing as much competition as possible between carriers and curbing abuses of monopoly powers as practiced by the railroads of the time. Over the years, regulations became more and more restrictive. "By the 1970s, there existed an elaborate and complex system of federal regulations that covered, usually in great detail, most aspects of railroad operations."[3] By the post–World War II era, the major elements of regulation included some specific provisions.

Controlled Expansion of a Railroad's Territory

Permission was needed from the Interstate Commerce Commission (ICC) to expand a railroad's operating territory. For example, regulators needed to approve the expansion of the Union Pacific Railroad into the Powder River Basin in Montana and Wyoming in 1982. The Burlington Northern Railway was already serving the territory and objected to having a new competitor. A third railroad, the Dakota, Minnesota and Eastern Railroad (DM&E) also obtained permission to extend its line into the Basin despite strong objections from other railroads. In the end, the capital requirements for expanding the railroad right of way proved a significant barrier, and the project was dropped when the DM&E was acquired by the Canadian Pacific Railway. The bottom line was that a railroad could not enter new markets without permission from the ICC. In addition, the financial barriers and the fact that other railroads would object to such expansions made the task all the more difficult.

Although still difficult in a regulatory environment, the way to expand a railroad's operating territory was through merger and acquisition. The merger of the PRR and the NYC into the Penn Central (1968) was the first significant merger in the period before deregulation. The merger was characterized as a side-by-side merger, that is, two parallel railroads. Such mergers are normally justified by savings generated by the elimination of duplicate facilities. The hope was the flow of savings would make both carriers healthy. The challenge for the ICC in such cases is that competition is reduced per se, as well as reductions in service and the loss of jobs. The justification for such mergers often hinged on invoking a failing business doctrine. That is, if the merger is not allowed, neither carrier will survive and the public will be harmed more severely. The Penn Central eventually declared bankruptcy in 1970 and disappeared in 1976 with the reorganization of the northeast railroads into Conrail.[4]

More relevant to the Grand Trunk, or similar regional carriers, was the idea of an end-to-end merger. An end-to-end merger, such as the Grand Trunk and the Chicago, Milwaukee, St. Paul and Pacific Railroad (Milwaukee Road), presents much less of a challenge for the ICC. The extension of two lines will improve or maintain service, preserve jobs, and generally have a positive reception from the public. Objections to this type of merger often come from competing carriers who fear a lessening of competitive position. The opportunity for such mergers often occur when one of the connecting lines becomes financially challenged. The justification for such mergers often rests on the financial resources that the stronger carrier can devote to healing its new partner. This logic played out in spades in the eventual merger of the Milwaukee Road. A more recent example of this process occurred in 1999 when CSX and Norfolk Southern divided up the troubled Conrail system.[5]

Controlled Exit from Markets

The prime example of the attitude of the ICC toward abandonments was its reluctance to allow railroads to get out of the passenger business in a timely fashion.[6] It was considered important by the ICC to preserve service to smaller communities, which had no other service, even though it was clearly unprofitable for the railroads. However, passenger service wasn't the only thing that needed to be abandoned. From the very beginning of the twentieth century, the railroad system was overbuilt, and the number of railroad miles had been declining since 1916.[7] This meant that, over time, many of the branch lines that served a number of industries eventually turned unprofitable as those industries failed, went out of business or simply moved on. For example, as forests were depleted or reclamation costs made mines uneconomic, the remaining traffic did not justify the maintenance or minimum service required. It was not until the Staggers Act of 1980 that railroads had the opportunity to efficiently shed themselves of unprofitable branch lines. In many cases, such abandonments represented the formation of new shortline railroads that weren't required to operate under the same regulatory burden as their larger brethren.

Rates Need to be Reasonable, Public, and Non-discriminatory

One test of the reasonableness of a rate was if it was compensatory for the carrier, and the ultimate arbitrator of reasonableness was the ICC. The ICC generally used a methodology that compared the proposed rate to existing rates for similar commodities, distances, etc. One of the effects of regulation was that rate levels were ultimately maintained to allow every carrier that wanted to compete for the traffic to make some money. The low-cost carrier might establish the rate on a fully allocated cost basis while other carriers, in order to be competitive, would match the rate and take a lesser contribution to its bottom line. Since rail transportation was often considered a commodity, there was very little differentiation based on price in the marketplace. This lack of price competition was enforced by requiring that every rate be made public. Industrial shippers buying rail services employed staff who constantly monitored the rates paid by their competitors. If one was at a disadvantage, the organization would begin negotiating with the relevant railroad(s) to equalize the two shippers. Publication of rates also made it difficult for railroads to discriminate between shippers. In a broad sense, all of a railroad's customers needed to be treated in a similar fashion, regardless of size. This meant that it was difficult for railroads to create special services for its largest shippers; service became homogeneous between competing railroads.

Within this environment, it was difficult for railroads to differentiate themselves. For the first fifty years of regulation, the financial barriers to entry led railroads to believe that they had a natural market where shippers had limited options. Throughout the 1970s, it was a fair assessment that railroads primarily competed with each other rather than other modes of transportation. The emphasis was on being the low-cost provider. Operating departments generally tried to perform as efficiently as possible but not for the particular convenience of the shipper. Traffic (sales) departments resisted changing rates for fear of having to lower rates to other shippers. As a result, the most common sales strategy for increasing business was to convince shippers to include their railroad in the shipment's routing.[8] By the same token, a railroad needed to protect its share of business from being rerouted to competing carriers. The tools for accomplishing these tasks were often "gifts" for the decision makers in the shipper's firm.

Looking at the railroad landscape starting in the 1970s, there was already a pattern of dominant and regional railroads. The latter depended on connections to survive and were ripe for merger after Staggers. The formation of Conrail (1976), which replaced the Penn Central and other bankrupt railroads, dominated the Northeast. The csx system was formed in 1980 by combining Chessie System and the Seaboard Coast Line Railroad (scl).[9] The scl had already acquired the Louisville and Nashville Railroad (l&n), and the Chessie System had already combined the Baltimore and Ohio Railroad (b&o) with the Chesapeake and Ohio (c&o), giving csx a major presence in both the north and Southeast. The gtw and the Detroit, Toledo and Ironton Railroad (dt&i) faced being left out in the cold since most of their business depended on connecting traffic from the newly merged lines. For example, the merger of larger carriers was typically followed by attempts to close interchanges with connecting carriers in order to eliminate alternate routings of traffic. Once the csx system absorbed the l&n, the merged carriers could encourage shippers not to use routings involving the gtw. On the one hand, gtw needed to preserve its competitive position by objecting to the merger of competitive railroads. On the other hand, it needed to find merger partners of its own.

In a similar vein, the so-called Northern Lines Merger which combined the Great Northern, Northern Pacific and Spokane Portland & Seattle Railways with the Chicago, Burlington and Quincy Railroad to form the Burlington Northern Railway (BN) in 1968 represented significant competition for the Union Pacific and dominated the Milwaukee Road between Chicago and the Pacific Northwest. As will be discussed later, the weakened Milwaukee Road was an important element of John Burdakin's growth strategy for the Grand Trunk.

POST STAGGERS: 1980 AND BEYOND

It is difficult to overstate the massive paradigm shift brought on by the Staggers Act of 1980. Staggers made most of the pre-existing limits of regulation moot. The major changes included the ability to make confidential rate contracts with specific shippers. Rates could be tailored for the precise needs of an individual shipper without fear of extending it to all competitors. Rates didn't have to be public although they still needed to be approved by the ICC. Service efficiencies and market forces could be used to justify rates that discriminated between competitors. Selling railroad services quickly switched from a solicitation to a marketing strategy.

Under Staggers, mergers were almost encouraged in recognition of the fact that regulation had damaged the well-being of the industry. As noted, railroad management recognized the need to become larger and control both origin and destination of a shipment. This presented a number of challenges for the Grand Trunk. The GTW was owned by the Canadian National Railway (CN), which was a Crown Corporation[10] and had a hands-off philosophy about its U.S. subsidiaries. The notion was that the U.S. subsidiaries were to do no harm to CN in exchange for freedom of management. By the same token, CN would not be a source of deep pockets for Grand Trunk.

The bottom line was that the CN would need to be strongly convinced of the value of any proposed merger.

After Staggers, shippers were becoming more aggressive in terms of seeking rate relief. The Grand Trunk's primary originating market was the automobile industry, in particular General Motors. The demands for both service improvements and rate relief from the automotive industry were made all the more powerful by the fact that automotive traffic was also subject to competition from a well-developed trucking industry. Post deregulation would bring substantial downward pressure on rates and revenue brought on by an aggressive primary shipper and intermodal competition.[11]

The following pages attempt to share how John Burdakin negotiated the various evolutionary phases of railroad life while maintaining a strong family life. He learned his trade in a very traditional, hierarchal style of management and emerged as a creative leader in what became a very competitive industry. In addition, the reader will also notice how the sense of family, not just his own, entered into his decision-making process.

Important Dates in the Life of John H. Burdakin

August 11, 1922   Born in Milton, Massachusetts, to L. Richard and Martha Burdakin

May 1940   Graduated from North Quincy High School, Quincy, Massachusetts

September 1940   Began classes at Massachusetts Institute of Technology (MIT), Cambridge

April 1943   Called to active duty in U.S. Army; basic training and Officer Candidate School training at Fort Belvoir, Virginia

Summer 1944   Commissioned as second lieutenant, assigned to Corps of Engineers, training soldiers in surveying, basic training, and heavy equipment

October 1946   Discharged as first lieutenant from U.S. Army; starts senior year at MIT

June 1947   Graduates from MIT with degree in civil engineering

Summer 1947   Junior Engineer with Pennsylvania Railroad (PRR) at Penn Station in New York City;

	further training in Altoona, Pennsylvania, and Lewistown, Pennsylvania
Summer 1948	First supervisory job, Assistant Supervisor Track, branch line, Jamesburg, New Jersey
October 2, 1948	Marries Jean Moulton at her parents' home in Milton, Massachusetts
Late fall, 1948	Assistant Supervisor Track, main line, Coshocton, Ohio
1951	Track Supervisor, branch line, Camden, New Jersey
July 24, 1952	Son John Jr. born in Camden, New Jersey
1953	Track Supervisor, main line, Perryville, Maryland
March 10, 1955	Son David born in Havre de Grace, Maryland
1955	Assistant District Engineer, Philadelphia
1958	Assistant Trainmaster, Louisville
March 12, 1959	Son Dan born in Louisville
1959	Assistant Trainmaster, Cincinnati
1960–61	Takes leave of absence to manage Railroad Division, Panama Railroad, Cristóbal, Canal Zone, for fifteen months
1961	Manager of Transportation Engineering, PRR Corporate Headquarters, Philadelphia
1963	Superintendent of Transportation, Baltimore, and then Regional Manager, Buffalo, New York
1965	General Superintendent, Eastern Region, Philadelphia, and then Assistant General Manager, Central Region, Pittsburgh
February 1, 1968	Penn Central formed with merger of PRR and New York Central
1968	Regional Manager, Penn Central Lakes Region, Cleveland

January 1970	Vice President and General Manager, Penn Central Northern Region, Detroit; resigned in June 1971
July 1971	Vice President Operations, Grand Trunk Western Railroad, Detroit
1974	President, Grand Trunk Western Railroad, with presidencies of Duluth, Winnipeg & Pacific Railway; Central Vermont Railway; and Grand Trunk Corporation added in 1975
1986	Vice Chairman, Grand Trunk Corporation; Grand Trunk board member
1987	Retires; remains in Michigan, with winters in Naples, Florida
2010	John and Jean Burdakin move from Michigan to Colorado
March 30, 2012	Jean Burdakin dies of pancreatic cancer
October 2013	John Burdakin moves to Cedar Rapids, Iowa
September 11, 2014	John Burdakin dies at age ninety-two

The Durand (Michigan) Union Depot now houses a community center and the Michigan Railroad History Museum. John Burdakin sold the Grand Trunk Western depot to the city for $1 in 1979. (Photo courtesy of the Michigan Railroad History Museum)

John Burdakin stands outside the new Grand Trunk repair shop in Wisconsin, which he made possible with the sale of Grand Trunk property in Duluth, Minnesota. (Photo from John H. Burdakin collection)

CHAPTER 1

WHEN PUT IN CHARGE,

TAKE CHARGE

BOSSES SET THE TONE, GOALS, AND EXPECTATIONS. WHEN NAMED TO head the Grand Trunk Western (GTW), a railroad bleeding red ink, John Burdakin listened, streamlined operations, and invested in railway track, equipment, and employee training. He improved safety and communications, and enforced the rules fairly and consistently. Slowly—and with a lot of help from others—pride in the workplace began to grow, and profits began to replace losses.

"You get respect back if you give it," Burdakin says. "If I'm going to tell you what to do, that respect has to be there. Nothing can be gained by me acting like your buddy. A boss doing that is going to be taken advantage of." Burdakin believes managers must be competent, confident, and honest. When asked a question, they should answer it as fully and truthfully as they can, though withholding information, if not asked for it directly, is sometimes the wisest course. When employees ask about their future in your company, tell them truthfully where they stand. When labor digs in its heels, negotiate. Work with your people, but when put in charge, take charge. Say what you expect of other employees and of the company.

Burdakin recalls one manager who was called "Mumbles" behind his back because no one could fully understand what he was saying or what he wanted. "I never did decide if it was his Virginia accent or on purpose, but many employees would be stopping by my office, asking me what he really meant or what he really wanted."

Bosses, he notes, must be clear in their communications. "How can you expect people to know what your game plan is, what you're trying to accomplish, if you don't tell them clearly what you're thinking?" he says. "You may find out, in the process, that your thinking is wrong. Maybe your managers can fine-tune the direction you're thinking about, put on the track shoes instead of the lead shoes."

EARLY DEMONSTRATIONS OF LEADERSHIP

The recognition of Burdakin's abilities as a manager started when he was working for the Pennsylvania Railroad (PRR) in Philadelphia. A steelworkers' strike had shut down all the steel mills. Ships loaded with iron ore, from as far away as Newfoundland, Africa, and South America, continued arriving at the port of South Philadelphia. The ore had to be unloaded so the ships could return for more ore. When all of the railroad's hopper cars were filled, the ore was trucked away and stored on railroad property.

Burdakin's bosses, he says, made a "battlefield promotion," naming him the "General Manager of Ore in Storage," to basically serve as a buffer between the dock foreman, named "Big George" Johnson, and the railroad's front office. "Big George" knew the railroad's president and vice president of operations from previous assignments and would not hesitate to call them when something went wrong. "My job," Burdakin says, "was to keep 'Big George' or his people from bothering the top officers on the PRR. I spent considerable time on the docks and became acquainted with everyone there, even playing chess with dockworkers on their lunch hour."

Burdakin was concerned the ore not be stacked too high, given that the ground was swampy and the dock could shift. He learned, though, that iron ore can survive in any weather, even under water, commenting, "You learn something every day!" Even though he wasn't told to, Burdakin also kept track of how many tons of ore were being stored on the ground, so the railroad could collect the correct storage fee—one dollar per ton per month. "They knew I was watching," Burdakin says. "I wanted them to know I was watching." Eventually, the storage rental fee paid for the thirty to forty trucks the railroad used each day to transport the ore from the dock to the storage area. And Burdakin proved his ability to organize and run a project—to take charge when put in charge.

TAKING CHARGE AT GRAND TRUNK WESTERN

The years of training and management experience at the Pennsylvania Railroad/Penn Central came to fruition when Robert A. Bandeen, as president of GTW; Duluth, Winnipeg & Pacific (DWP); and Central Vermont (CV), in 1971, hired Burdakin as vice president of operations for the Grand Trunk Western Railroad. In 1974, Bandeen became president and CEO of the Canadian National (CN).[1] In that year, Bandeen named Burdakin the president of GTW. A year later, he named Burdakin as president of the DWP and CV Railways, as well as the Grand Trunk Corporation (GTC).[2] Burdakin, with Bandeen's support, would "run the show" for the next ten years.[3]

The GTW, headquartered in Detroit, was a subsidiary of Canadian National, the government-owned railroad headquartered in Montreal. The U.S. operations were known as CN's "ugly stepchild" and as the last stop for managers before retirement or an initial stop for new managers being groomed for bigger responsibilities. It had always bled red ink, which CN absorbed, until it reached the point that company officers feared the losses would come to the attention of the *Toronto Globe and Mail*. It would be an embarrassment if the newspaper reported the number of Canadian dollars being spent to support U.S. operations.

Bandeen was determined to bring GTW up to the standards of modern U.S. railroads and have it establish its own U.S. identity and, he hoped, lessen the red ink and possibly even turn a profit. He hired Burdakin, who had been running Penn Central's Northern Region in Detroit, to oversee Grand Trunk operations. He also hired two other vice presidents: Walter H. Cramer in marketing and Donald G. Wooden in finance and corporate planning.[4]

"At the time, Grand Trunk was about five years behind the times everywhere," Burdakin says. "Bandeen had the right idea to Americanize the U.S. operations. He was not one who wanted instant returns or great profits. He felt the best thing was little improvements in many different places, in many different ways. He wasn't driven—thus we weren't driven—to make the most money we could. If Grand Trunk was going to make profits by abandoning railroads or ignoring maintenance and track improvements, I would have stayed with Penn Central, even though the management people there were tearing the railroad apart. We wanted to improve the Grand Trunk, step by step, in a logical way. My feeling was that the money will come along if you have a company that is running well."

The first thing Burdakin did in his new job was "to get out, see the railroad, and meet the people. Whenever I came across a track gang or an engine crew, I would stop, get out and shake their hands, and introduce myself as the new vice president. At least they knew what I looked like and hopefully could get a little confidence in their own minds of what my vision of the Grand Trunk should be."

Burdakin says he found the Grand Trunk had competent managers, but ones who were in the habit of waiting for their Canadian supervisors to tell them what to do. "I didn't think that was the way to run a railroad," Burdakin says. "I wanted the initiative of all the managers, wanted them thinking every day about how to improve their piece of the railroad. I wanted them to pick up the reins and start driving their own horse. Nobody at the time was thinking critically about whether something was needed or not."

William Litfin Sr., who spent his entire career in operations with GTW, made up his mind about the kind of "take-charge" leader Burdakin was in 1971, only a few months after Burdakin had been named the railroad's vice president of operations. He first met Burdakin in Pontiac, Michigan, after two trains had collided, causing fires and loss of life.

"John showed up immediately and started coordinating what to do—talking to the press, getting engines moved, getting cars picked up," Litfin says. "He didn't know anyone. We were a bunch of strangers. But he coordinated everything really well. He never got mad, he never hollered. When a situation started falling apart, he put it back together. I was impressed by his dedication and knowledge. And from that time on, I was impressed with him."

Another early example of leadership came at Port Huron, Michigan, where Burdakin and a transportation team found five carpenters replacing the roof on a small building adjacent to a siding. Burdakin asked what the building was used for. The answer: To house livestock when they had to be taken off freight cars "to be fed and watered" in compliance with federal law. How often was the building used? Burdakin asked, noting he couldn't recall seeing cattle in Grand Trunk railcars. No one knew. It took three days to get the answer, which no one really wanted to share with the new boss. The building had been used once in the past five years, for one horse. And that horse hadn't been on a train; it had been on a truck that Canadian officials had refused entry to. So the GTW building had been pressed into service. The next question from Burdakin: Can marketing get us out of the agreement that requires such a facility? The answer, eventually, was yes.[5]

"So that was one thing we didn't have to worry about any longer," Burdakin says. "But that was the type of thinking going on at Grand Trunk when I first arrived."

Burdakin and Bill Glavin, his new chief engineer, then set about eliminating GTW buildings that duplicated others or were unnecessary. Every toolhouse, for example, had separate lavatory facilities for the trackmen and the signalmen. Why not consolidate those facilities? Together, Burdakin and Glavin eliminated more than 160 buildings the first year, ranging from outhouses to a four-story, multipurpose brick building at Port Huron. The consolidations saved money and maintenance costs, a step in the right direction.

In Durand, Michigan, however, the railroad ran into resistance from local citizens when it announced plans to raze the brick train station. "So we sold it to the community, where it still serves as a town center. The old station also houses the Michigan Railroad Museum," Burdakin says. "So that worked out well for all concerned."

Burdakin and Glavin also closed a carpenter's shop that had specialized in replacing the molding in Grand Trunk buildings. "This was the kind of molding you could buy at a lumberyard," Burdakin says. "We put the carpenters outside, working on bridges and other properties, rather than sitting around a shop, spending quite a bit of time thinking about moldings."

Another thing that Burdakin changed "almost instantaneously" at Grand Trunk was the system used for promotions and transfers, which was controlled "almost 100 percent" by the Personnel Department. "If any manager had a vacancy and needed to promote someone, it was left to the Personnel Department to do it," Burdakin says. "Those promotions and transfers were announced by Personnel on the last Friday of every month. Everyone involved lived in fear of those Fridays, fearing they might be relocated. Where I came from, the person in charge who had a vacancy had a major say in the replacement. A trainmaster, for example, picked the assistant trainmaster, with the help of the Personnel Department, but not Personnel independently. It was important to me that the person responsible for the territory be able to select the people who were going to fill a vacancy."

Burdakin also changed the compensation model that relied on how many dollars and how many employees managers managed. Those managing the most dollars and the most employees earned the most money. That model, Burdakin says, worked against efficiencies.

"If your salary as a manager was going to be reduced if you reduced your workforce, where's the incentive?" Burdakin says. "That went against my principles. If I had to reduce the workforce, I wanted my managers to do that, and I didn't want them thinking of their job level first."

At the same time, Burdakin encouraged his managers to "see what the rest of the world was like" and to attend and participate in meetings of professional organizations. GTW managers had seldom gone to such meetings. "I told them they were expected to attend such gatherings, if invited," Burdakin says. "How can you find out what other railroads are doing without having lunch with them? What are their problems? What advice do they have on solving your problems?" The bonus: When you go, take your wife—again, if she is invited and wants to go—"and let her associate with her peers. Surprisingly, the spouses would frequently find out those people with big titles from large carriers weren't as knowledgeable as the people we had at Grand Trunk. It also helped them understand the fifteen-hour days and midnight telephone calls that were sometimes necessary. I wanted them to know they were a key partner, that they were important to the team." The second bonus: GTW would even pay for a babysitter, if needed, so the couple could attend professional meetings together.

Burdakin says it didn't take long before most employees seemed "to take more interest in what we and they were doing. People were coming up with ideas, thinking about how their jobs could be done better and at less expense. What new equipment did they need? It was my job to find a way to get them the tools they needed to operate efficiently."

The changes apparently impressed a lot of people and motivated them to work more productively and make GTW a better railroad. One manager, Warren Brown, for example, pushed ahead with his plan to provide radio service from one end of GTW to the other. Burdakin made it happen, putting up five communication towers between Chicago and Detroit, and radios replaced telephones, eliminating the poles and wires along each track.

Burdakin also saw to it that air-conditioning was installed at GTW's ten-story, fifty-year-old office building in downtown Detroit. Before air-conditioning, office employees were sent home when the temperature and humidity reached a certain point on hot summer days. On such days, Burdakin recalls with a smile, the main activity seemed to be checking the thermometer.

In another example of leadership, longtime GTW executive Howard M. Tischler discovered that *Fortune* magazine was not including GTC in its annual list of the nation's fifty largest transportation companies. The magazine had never seen GTC financials. The statements were sent, and GTC was ranked in the high forties on *Fortune's* list.

LABOR RELATIONS

One of the biggest problems that Burdakin faced at GTW was labor relations. "There was no communication between labor and management. There was no trust either way," he says. As an example, he relates how some clerks in Pontiac, Michigan, unhappy with the new keypunch machines they felt threatened their jobs, had taken to slipping sand into the machines. The sand interfered with the punch cards that were tracking GTW freight and its all-important service to the Detroit auto plants. "I knew," Burdakin says, "I had to find some way to communicate with the families, the wives, as well as the workers, to make sure they're happy with their jobs and what's going on in the company, so they'll respond appropriately when I changed the things I knew needed to be changed."

One of the points of common agreement was employee safety. Burdakin also moved to improve employee morale and to clean up railroad properties. Finding GTW track in better condition than that of many carriers, the railroad advertised itself as the "Good Track Road." The black locomotives were painted a medium blue—immediately dubbed "Burdakin Blue," a designation Burdakin wasn't fond of but lived with. Things just looked better and more modern.

In 1971, when Burdakin arrived at GTW as vice president of operations, he discovered GTW crews were to be paid for a week's work even though rail traffic was at a virtual standstill between Christmas and New Year's when Detroit's automobile plants shut down for the holidays. He met with labor leadership and said he could not afford to pay crew salaries with no work to do, and that he was going to furlough crews for that week. Labor responded with pickets—including one sign that read "Burdakin Kills Santa *Cluas*." (To this day, Burdakin recalls the picket sign correctly spelled his name but misspelled Claus.) The union threatened that workers would be late coming back to work after the forced furlough.

Burdakin kept negotiating with the union and finally achieved agreement: Those who worked the day before the Christmas layoff and then came back to work the day after the furlough would receive one day's bonus pay. Importantly, the union agreed that workers would return to their previous positions, eliminating any need for the seniority bidding process that would be expensive and time-consuming, and would cause delays as workers moved into new jobs. The furlough still wasn't popular, but the settlement met Burdakin's fiduciary responsibilities as manager of a company where old ways had to change.

"When you're the boss, some people won't always like what you're going to do," he says. "You have to get past that."

While he was at it, Burdakin also ended the Grand Trunk tradition of letting all office employees off work at noon on Christmas Eve. Many would gather at restaurants, and a few would overindulge, including one accounting employee who wobbled home, knocked over his family's Christmas tree, and then went to bed. "You can imagine the impact on the family's Christmas celebration," Burdakin says. "I went home thinking about GTW's part in ruining a family's celebration of Christmas and was determined this wasn't going to be repeated on my watch."

And so it came to be that GTW employees stayed in the office on Christmas Eve and joined in departmental luncheons (without alcohol). They brought snacks and finger foods from home, and GTW donated a bit toward the luncheon expense. Office employees then were allowed to go home a bit early, in early to midafternoon.

"My 'forced' luncheon with fellow employees was a great success in many ways, at an expense of only two dollars—later three dollars—per employee," Burdakin says. "It got people talking to each other."

Another change Burdakin implemented at Grand Trunk concerned trainmen who'd been dismissed during the year because they were visibly intoxicated or caught drinking at work, thereby violating "Rule G."[6] The men—usually four to five a year—were put on the "Christmas list" and offered their jobs back effective January 1, "just because it was Christmas." "I'd never heard of such a thing," Burdakin says, "but it had been standard procedure at Grand Trunk."

Burdakin asked the Grand Trunk labor relations manager if the unions would vouch that the fired workers had changed their ways. "I couldn't see rehiring someone and possibly going through that whole firing procedure again in the next year or two," Burdakin says. "Those workers knew what

9

was going to happen if they were intoxicated at work or caught drinking while on the job. I sent the labor relations manager out the door with the Christmas list, and he looked like a whipped dog. He had to go back to the union and say, 'It isn't going to happen this year.' I might have changed my mind if a fellow was in Alcoholics Anonymous or had changed his ways, but I didn't hear any such support."

And then, in 1972, came an assist from Santa Claus. Art Fettig, the former Grand Trunk claims agent Burdakin had promoted to employee communications officer, was talking to the safety officer at the Detroit, Toledo & Ironton Railroad, about DT&I's "Santa Train." He learned DT&I employees decorated a train and caboose at Christmas and invited orphans aboard for treats and gifts. Fettig took the idea and expanded it to a Santa Train that would tour the Grand Trunk line, with the top Grand Trunk executives and their families on board.[7] Railroad employees, their families, and neighbors would be invited on board to meet the brass—and Santa. Burdakin embraced the idea. Three passenger cars, including the president's inspection car, and a locomotive made up the train. The Port Huron Car Shops built a big spot in the back of the president's car for Santa to sit and greet little ones. Train crews volunteered their time to run the Santa Train, though Burdakin insisted they be paid. Other workers donated snacks and helped decorate the cars. Fettig added slide shows and pamphlets about the Grand Trunk and railroad safety. Christmas music played. The Christmas tree "talked," conversing with the children as they waited in line to see Santa. The Santa Train stopped at Grand Trunk's major terminals on the two weekends before Christmas. It traveled from Port Huron to Flint to Lansing and then on to Chicago where it tied up for the night. The next morning, the Chicago employees visited Santa, and then it was on to South Bend and then Battle Creek with its big locomotive shops. The second weekend included a stop at Birmingham for Detroit employees and then Pontiac, where Burdakin had been warned the train might find pickets because of ongoing labor disputes. There were no pickets, just a big, smiling crowd.

"It was a revealing moment for me to realize that Mr. Burdakin recognized that he might be personally embarrassed implementing new concepts, but he was brave enough to move on," Fettig recalls. "We could have avoided the Pontiac stop, but that was where the real labor problems were, and Mr. Burdakin insisted we go where the action was."

Burdakin adds, "Most of the people we met had never seen a railroad president or vice president, let alone his wife, or even the inside of a passenger car." One man, he says, couldn't believe he'd shaken hands with railroad royalty. "He won't wash his hand for a week," the man's wife said. One woman brought her fourteen-day-old baby because she wanted the baby to see Santa.

The effort "did its job," Burdakin says. "We didn't have animosity between labor and management from that point on. The Canadian National management, up to that point, had pretty much been a 'do-as-I-say' operation. Managers weren't accustomed to talking to workmen and the people who swept the floors and performed other necessary jobs but who weren't necessarily engineers or conductors or who had jobs with titles. We opened up communication fabulously with the Santa Train. It helped families understand why you sometimes had to work all night. It also helped insofar as safety awareness. It paid off." The Santa Train, though scaled back in recent years, is still running.

In a further effort to improve communication and morale, Burdakin supported a monthly newsletter that was mailed to each employee's home. The *GT Reporter* was a professionally produced publication, Burdakin says, one that built pride among Grand Trunk employees and kept their families informed about what Mom or Dad and the company were doing. To further cement communication with employees, Burdakin summed up Grand Trunk's corporate goals and mailed the information to each employee's home. It was an innovative idea. Company objectives had not been conveyed in that fashion before. In simple, straightforward language, Burdakin in 1975 set forth his vision for GTW, detailing eight goals that would guide him and GTW employees throughout his tenure.

- To direct the activities of the company so as to achieve a long-term profitable position reflecting an adequate return on assets and to attain fiscal stability and independence in terms of cash for operating and capital expenditures. These activities will recognize Canadian National's interest at all times.

- To provide competitive services, facilities, prices, and equipment where financially and otherwise feasible to fulfill the needs of our present and potential customers.
- To use all reasonable means to promote and provide safe operating conditions so as to minimize personal injuries and property losses to employees, customers, and the general public.
- To adequately maintain the physical plant and equipment while adopting technological improvements when they are in concert with these objectives.
- To provide employees with a working environment that will ensure equal employment opportunities, competitive wages and benefits, competent and motivating supervision, and opportunities for job satisfaction and advancement in surroundings conducive to good performance and achievement.
- To develop and maintain an organization and personnel capable of providing and perpetuating able management and a competent workforce.
- To conduct business in a socially responsible manner, being mindful of the role of the company as a desirable member of the community and the state.
- To enhance the image of the company and the industry in the eyes of the government, the community, the public, and our employees.

THE CN-GTW MANAGEMENT TEAM

Grand Trunk Western had lost money for more than twenty straight years; then, under Burdakin's leadership, it had eight straight years of profits, from 1973 through 1981. By 1977, all three railroads that were part of the Grand Trunk Corporation made money—an almost unimaginable improvement. Burdakin is quick to share credit with the Grand Trunk management team and, in particular, the leadership of the man he considered his mentor,

Robert Bandeen. Bandeen was president of Canadian National from 1974 to 1982, reorganizing and streamlining the Crown Corporation—meaning the Canadian government owned the huge railroad—into a profitable operation. After leaving Canadian National, Bandeen undertook similar changes at Crown Life, an insurance company, before he retired in 1985. The son of an Ontario tobacco farmer and elementary school teacher, Bandeen excelled in school and earned a PhD in economics from Duke University. He and his wife, Mona, were major supporters of the arts in Canada. After their initial lunch, where Bandeen met and hired Burdakin, Burdakin says he came away confident that Bandeen would be president of Canadian National and could even be prime minister of Canada, if he wished. He was that impressive.

THE CONFIDENCE TO LEAD

So, when put in charge, how does one have the confidence to actually take charge? Burdakin believes leadership starts with competence—knowing what you're talking about—followed by confidence.

He believes his ability to command started in his days as a patrol leader in Boy Scouts and when, as a teenager, he was racing his fifteen-and-a-half-foot snipe-class sailboat in the Boston Harbor. On that sailboat, he was completely in charge. He sanded it, painted it, bought and rigged its sails, and commanded its crew (himself and a friend) on race days. "I didn't realize at the time what an educational process it was," he says.

Burdakin's leadership grew during the three years he was in the Reserve Officers' Training Corps (ROTC) at MIT, and, after he was called to active duty by the army, he gained more experience in Officer Candidate School and then as a second lieutenant during World War II when he trained draftees.

Men in the Burdakin line had served in many of the nation's wars, starting with the Civil War, so "military service was kind of expected," he says. "I don't recall even discussing it with my parents."

At the time Burdakin entered MIT, in 1940, ROTC training was required of all MIT freshmen and sophomores. He signed up for advanced ROTC in his junior and senior years because it offered a small stipend. He received a medal for being the top student in the engineering program and was chosen to lead the fifty-three MIT engineering students called to active duty in April 1943.

The famed Burdakin confidence showed itself early on when the recruits were en route to Fort Belvoir in Virginia. The recruits left one Sunday from the North Station in Boston, with the MIT students assigned to their own coach car.

"The only thing I can remember about that trip from Boston is that it was very hot, and we removed our heavy khaki shirts," Burdakin relates. "That brought the MP [military police], with orders to put our shirts back on. I argued with them. They realized that the heat—and the fact that we had a separate car—made it acceptable for us to keep our shirts off to cope with the heat."

When he was in training to be an officer, Burdakin recalls, it was his turn to lead his platoon from lunch to the next class. A tactical training officer marched alongside the platoon, yelling at Burdakin, attempting to break his thought process. It didn't work. Burdakin kept his platoon in step and delivered a full-volume blast in the tactical officer's ear. Lesson learned: Volume has its place in dealing with "excited" people.

After graduating from Officer Candidate School and being commissioned as a second lieutenant, Burdakin trained recently inducted draftees and then was in charge of air-compressor and crane training. With the Corps of Engineers, he trained soldiers on heavy equipment and surveying.

"You find out that you can direct people and that people will listen to you," Burdakin says. "You learn to say what you want and not to 'smooth' it over too much. Of course, I respected my superiors, but I never felt inferior or intimidated by rank, position, or education, be it applying for a job, shaking hands with supervisors, or even the president. I never understood people 'shaking in their boots' about seeing the boss. I'd state my case and let the chips fall where they may. It's likely the way I was raised—that you're equal to other people. In turn, I hope that I treated others fairly and equally."

At the end of the war, the colonel of the Second Engineer Training Group singled out Burdakin for a commendation, citing his initiative, intelligence, and hard work. Burdakin, knowing that the number of commendations was limited and that he was headed back to MIT, politely declined the recognition, suggesting the colonel give the commendation to someone who was going to make a career of the military.

One of Burdakin's great strengths throughout his subsequent career was his ability to communicate to others, regardless of their station in life. His childhood in a middle-class neighborhood outside Boston taught him how to talk to (and respect) blue-collar workers. He could talk to trainmen and porters as well as presidents and CEOs.

That ability to "network"—before that term gained currency—served Burdakin and his railroads well. He brought in new ideas and experts. He sent his managers to national conferences and to the Harvard Business Management School. A purchasing agent once told Burdakin he wouldn't go on a golf outing because it was hosted by supply salespeople. The man didn't want it to appear he was being unduly influenced in purchasing decisions.

"You can learn more hitting a golf ball and sitting around talking to people than you can sitting at home alone, talking to yourself," Burdakin told the man, adding he was confident the man's decisions could not be swayed by a round of golf.

Another leadership tip from Burdakin: Keep notes. Early on, Burdakin developed the habit of writing down stories or sayings on 3-by-5-inch index cards. He could pull out a few of those cards and be ready for a speech or program or even saying grace before a meal. Those notes, he says, were particularly helpful early in his career when he wasn't accustomed to public speaking. It's a tip that's easily adapted these days to a computer or a smart phone folder.

And, finally, he encourages managers to listen to their people and learn from them. When Burdakin was beginning his career with the Pennsylvania Railroad, he was working with Carl McGhee in Lewistown, Pennsylvania. McGhee had risen through the ranks as a trackman, foreman, general foreman, and then to supervisor of track responsible for about fifty miles of the mainline between Harrisburg and Pittsburgh. The three or four tracks carried heavy passenger and freight traffic.

One day, Burdakin was assigned to "string line" the westbound main line under the coal dock, realigning the track's curves to take out the kinks and rough spots. Burdakin confessed his world-class engineering education at MIT had not covered string lining. McGhee's response: "Take George with you. He'll show you how it's done." George Sheetz was an all-around handyman. He'd had about eight years of schooling before he had to quit and get a job supporting his family after his father was crippled in a coal mining accident. In string lining, you take a 31-foot-long string and measure the distance between the inside of the rail and the string (the middle coordinate) every 15½ feet around a curve. From those notes, and using a bit of addition and subtraction, the track can be moved in or out to make a uniform, smooth curve.

The lesson was delivered by Sheetz while he and Burdakin sat under an apple tree alongside the track on a beautiful day in May. "It was undoubtedly the nicest classroom I ever enjoyed," Burdakin says. "George taught me what, why, and how, and then, satisfied with our notes, we worked with the track gang to realign the curve and remove the irregularities. A westbound freight train tested our day's work by gliding around the curve with no rocking or rolling of the cars." That evening, while having dinner alone, Burdakin reflected on the day and the lesson. "The lesson had been presented as thoroughly and clearly as any lesson received in college or in the army," he says. "But the real lesson of the day was that not all smart people are college graduates."

Finally, as a manager you can't please everyone and will sometimes be thought of as a "spherical SOB"—engineer Burdakin's term for "any way you look at it." Your decisions, as a manager, will sometimes make you unpopular. In an experience that tweaked a few of his fellow managers, the Canadian National accounting people noticed that Burdakin had requested four additional hot box detectors in Grand Trunk's capital budget for the coming year. The scanners, in common use in the United States but not in Canada, indicated when the brass bearings in a freight car axle were overheating.[8] The train could be stopped before the axle failed and caused a fire and derailment.

Bandeen, CN's president, asked the other Canadian National managers why they weren't asking for any of the devices in *their* capital budgets.

Surely, he mused, such a problem was not just a concern in the United States. Being shown up like that didn't endear Burdakin—the new American manager—to his Canadian counterparts. But it's the kind of thing a good manager has to shrug off.

From similar experiences, Burdakin cautions managers—especially new managers—against becoming "buddies" with the people they supervise. "You can be respectful of your subordinates and even friendly, but you're the boss," he says. "I don't believe managers should be buddy-buddy or socializing with the staff after work."

"You also have to realize, as a boss, that people come to work, and you don't know what's going on in their lives," Burdakin adds. "Maybe they're having problems with their marriage or their children or their finances—things that can affect how they go about their work. You can't do much about those things. You can't make everybody happy."

TAKEAWAYS

- When put in the role of a decision maker, make decisions.
- Give your honest opinion on workplace issues and ideas. You're being paid for your thinking and your best judgment. That said, realize that sometimes the wisest course is to say nothing.
- Communicate. Keep your bosses informed. Share as much as possible with your employees.
- Ask questions. Listen to the answers. Consult. Act.
- Work is not high school. Being a boss is not a popularity contest.

John Burdakin at one of the many black-tie events he attended as president of the Grand Trunk Western Railroad. (Photo courtesy of Michigan Railroad History Museum)

John Burdakin with Michigan governor James Blanchard.
(Photo from John H. Burdakin collection)

CHAPTER 2

DO THE RIGHT THING

THERE ARE AT LEAST THREE REASONS WHY RULES ARE A WAY OF LIFE in the railroad industry. One is that oversight of employee performance is difficult since employees are beyond the view of the supervisors. Thus, there is a need for strict definition of responsibilities—that is, rules—in order to hold employees accountable. The second reason is that there is a strong labor-management culture in the railroad industry. Rules are used to define the boundaries of how management may discipline employees and labor will defend them. Finally, the emphasis on safety mandates the need for rules.

DO THE RIGHT THING

One of the early tests of Burdakin's "do-the-right-thing" mantra came in 1958 when the Pennsylvania Railroad (PRR) sent him to Louisville as assistant trainmaster on a branch line that provided freight service to two distilleries in the "Bend District" on the Ohio River. One of his first visitors was the manager of the Brown Forman Distillery, who was complaining he didn't get as many empty boxcars as his competitor, the Sunny Hill Distillery. Burdakin investigated and discovered Sunny Hill had been giving every PRR trainman a half-pint of whiskey every Friday. That little investment had been paying big dividends when the crews assigned the empty boxcars, with the majority and the better boxcars going to Sunny Hill. Burdakin says he went to Sunny Hill and asked that it stop the Friday practice.

"It didn't take long before I had a visit from a chap named Hy Moss, a conductor and the local union chairman," Burdakin recalls. The two walked around the roundhouse, "and I had to tell him why the men weren't getting any more bourbon—that they'd been playing favorites and they were stepping over the line. My standard was we treat all our customers equally. We got it straightened out, and somehow the favoritism vanished. I didn't have any more complaints."

John Burdakin had a somewhat similar experience after he became the vice president of operations for Grand Trunk Western in 1971. His boss, Robert A. Bandeen, came for a visit. Lunchtime arrived, and the boss suggested they send out for sandwiches and a beer. Burdakin, after taking a deep breath, decided to wade right in. "I'm sorry," he told the boss, "but we can't do that. Our policy is no liquor is allowed on railroad premises." Many years later, Burdakin says that, yes, "it was hard, when you're the new guy, to tell the boss who hired you that he couldn't have a beer. That does take intestinal fortitude. You do, after all, like your job. I'm not against bending an elbow, but not when on duty, on the premises, or where anyone else would be fired or suspended for having alcohol on-site. It was a rule I expected everyone to follow." Years later, one of Bandeen's sons told Burdakin's son John Jr. that Bandeen thought Burdakin "was the most honest man he had ever met." That, Burdakin says, "was, to me, a very large honor, a tremendous compliment, especially considering where it came from."

THE NEED TO BE FLEXIBLE

As a manager, John Burdakin was committed to following the rules. As an *exceptional* manager, John Burdakin realized that being flexible might be more important than strict adherence to protocols. Rules, he believes, can be violated, though one must be "extremely cautious" in making exceptions.

When Burdakin became the assistant trainmaster with the Pennsylvania Railroad in Cincinnati in 1959, he inherited a terminal in disarray.[1] Management and labor were at war. Cooperation was nonexistent. No one was talking. "Welcome to Cincinnati," John said to himself. As part of his orientation and to meet workers who'd never shaken hands with a trainmaster, Burdakin was touring the rail yards at night to introduce himself to second- and third-shift employees. Early one morning, at 2:30 A.M., he happened upon a roomful of trainmen playing poker in the basement of the Yard Office locker room when they should have been switching cars. The gambling was in clear violation of company rules.

Burdakin introduced himself, shaking hands with all the men, and asked them if they knew it was against the rules to be gambling while on duty. No response. Not knowing who the men were, Burdakin had each trainman put his "stamp" on a piece of paper—the stamps had the men's names and employee numbers on them—and then told them to go back to work.

The next morning the men's powerful union representative, Jimmy Gelease, beat Burdakin to his office. "Even before I could say, 'Good morning,' Jimmy asked me what I was going to do. I said truthfully I didn't know, but that I might be able to give him an answer later in the day."

Burdakin thought all day about what to do. "I needed to get their attention—that's for sure," Burdakin recalls thinking. "Did I really want to discipline all of these people? This problem was one I had inherited. Yes, I could fire them all, but think of the impact on their families and the need to train new employees. How could I get out the message that we would be working by the rule book?"

That afternoon, after work, Burdakin told Gelease he'd let the violation pass—this once. "If it happens again, your members won't get the same treatment," he told Gelease. "Then I delivered a strong lecture on how he

21

was as responsible for the men as I was, and that I was disappointed he'd allowed this to happen and that we needed to work together." As Gelease was turning to leave the meeting, Burdakin capped the surprising decision by giving Gelease the piece of paper with the employees' stamps on it. "You now have all my 'evidence.' Think it over." That decision, Burdakin says, "turned around the whole atmosphere of labor-management relations in the entire terminal. It was a major step forward, breaking down walls in one fell swoop."

In another experience with the PRR, around 1963, Burdakin wanted to make a roadway for trucks to use adjacent to the track south of Edgewood, Maryland. A bulldozer operator was following Burdakin's instructions when the dozer began to slide down the bank. To prevent the machine from flipping over, the operator (properly) put the dozer blade in the ground, but, in the process, it severed a buried cable.

All traffic on the Philadelphia–Washington line, including the "Morning Congressional" train, came to a halt for at least forty-five minutes. Everyone was upset, including the regional assistant chief engineer, who insisted Burdakin fire the bulldozer operator. "Since the operator was following my instructions, there was no way I could or would fire him," Burdakin says. He hoped the matter would die a natural death, but even after a month had passed, the inquiries continued. The assistant chief engineer *really* wanted the dozer operator fired. Burdakin decided he had to act, resorting to the major disciplinary action of an investigation and a trial.

Burdakin called in the dozer operator, making sure the man's union representative would be there, too. "I proceeded to recommend his dismissal without using the proper trial protocol, which I made sure his union rep noted. The rep was able to get the firing reversed by the regional Labor Relations Department on the basis of my 'error,' and the dozer operator remained employed. The operator did lose one day's pay, which he soon recovered with weekend overtime work I scheduled for him. A problem was averted, and a difficult situation managed."

Another time, early in Burdakin's career at the Pennsylvania Railroad as an assistant track supervisor, he found a track maintenance crew elevating the wrong rail on a reverse curve just west of Coshocton, Ohio—a serious mistake that could have caused a derailment. Burdakin checked to make sure no trains were coming and ordered the foreman to have the crew correct the elevation. "You know what's wrong, don't you?" he asked the foreman. "Well, *now* I do," the foreman responded. The track was fixed, and a possible tragedy averted.

Burdakin was left to puzzle out the right thing to do. "Do I tell my supervisor? We got out of it all right. All it's going to do is embarrass the section foreman. I ended up not saying anything to anybody," Burdakin recalls. "I sometimes regret that I didn't create a little 'school' right then and there so all the men would have known what they were doing wrong."

Lest one think from these examples that a key to Burdakin's management success was letting people get away with infractions—don't. These were the exceptions, but ones that illustrate the sense of fairness that informed Burdakin's management style and his belief (perhaps surprising in a beginning manager) that "workers do need an ombudsman" to protect them from capricious bosses.

THE VARIED RESPONSIBILITIES OF A TRAINMASTER

Another example of a tricky problem came early in Burdakin's career when he was assistant trainmaster at Louisville and was handling the special trains that came in from New York and from Chicago for the running of the Kentucky Derby. Everything was going smoothly, and all the trains had left the Pennsylvania Railroad yard except for the one carrying the PRR's vice president for the Western Region headquartered in Chicago.

"I was waiting for them to get out of town so I could go home. A tall, thin gentleman—he was the regional vice president—was standing on the platform of the office car, maybe wavering a bit," and called Burdakin over. "He told me that, in the course of the day, some of his guests had picked up a lady in Louisville and that she was on board the car, wanting to go to Chicago because she'd never ridden on an office car. 'We don't want her to go with us,' the vice president said. 'Can you get her off?' I said, 'I don't know, but I'll try.' The vice president responded, 'Get her off.' He was the vice president of one-third of the PRR, so I thought I'd better figure out how to do what he was asking without calling the police or making a scene, even though this was an area of life I had had no experience with."

Burdakin boarded the car and sat alongside the woman on a sofa, chit-chatting. "I figured I had to get her interested and invite her to spend time in Louisville. I told her a train ride to Chicago wasn't that much fun, you just sit there and bounce around. There's a lot more activity going on this evening right here at the Brown Hotel after the Derby. I let my hand grab her knee, and said, 'Why don't you stay here?' I never said 'we.' She said OK.

"So I escorted her off. As soon as my feet and her feet hit the ground, I motioned to the conductor to leave. So there I was. I have a new baby at home, my wife is there, and here I am, escorting a woman to the Brown Hotel. I found a taxi, opened the door, put her in, and threw a twenty-dollar bill in the front seat, telling the driver to take the lady wherever she wanted to go. I expect she was upset. But I got her off the railcar and went home to Jean. I didn't tell Jean about enticing the lady, with my hand on her knee, to go to the Brown Hotel for, I guess, ten years. That was the day I learned there are more things in the job description of assistant trainmaster than just moving boxcars."

THE NEED FOR HONESTY

Integrity is mentioned a lot when people talk about John Burdakin. It's a word with an elusive meaning, but when applied to Burdakin, it means honesty. It also means having the courage to speak the truth to power—especially when it would be easier to say nothing. "I'd say what I thought," Burdakin says. "Sometimes I'd keep my thoughts to myself, but I never uttered a false word. That's the way I was raised. My goal has been to live my life to benefit others, and as an example to others, by being unselfish, committed, and demonstrating integrity."

When Burdakin was working with Penn Central, right after the merger, in 1968, that made it the largest railroad in the United States,[2] Burdakin challenged the new Penn Central president/CEO, Alfred E. Perlman, when Perlman suggested railroads wouldn't need marketing departments if every car was delivered to the customer on time. Burdakin said he thought railroads needed marketing and salespeople to sell their services. A short debate ensued, with the CEO starting to become angry at being contradicted. Burdakin let it go, and that evening was invited on a walk with the new company's senior vice president. The man counseled Burdakin against contradicting Perlman. He repeated his advice—"Don't make the boss mad"—a half-dozen times, Burdakin recalls. Burdakin stayed with Penn Central three more years and witnessed firsthand what happens when a CEO doesn't want to hear bad news. "You learned that you couldn't trust what you were being told," he says. It was one of many disagreements he would have with top management decisions at Penn Central.

There was another example with Penn Central's merger with the New York, New Haven and Hartford Railroad (New Haven), which was primarily a passenger train operation. To receive Interstate Commerce Commission (ICC) approval for the Penn Central merger, the combined company had to take over the operations of the New Haven as early as 1965 and formally merged on January 1, 1969.[3] As a condition of the merger, Penn Central had to guarantee every employee at the smaller railroad a job for life. Burdakin told his boss the railroad could not make money on a passenger operation and advised Penn Central to walk away from the deal. But his boss declined to pass along that assessment, saying Perlman was set on the merger. "All the merger did was expedite the road's path to bankruptcy," Burdakin says. "Guaranteeing jobs for life was too heavy a load to carry."[4]

Burdakin later encountered one of those "guaranteed" jobs when he was at Grand Trunk and watched a Penn Central ticket agent typing at a speed that was, to be kind, glacial. "Is that the fastest you can type?" Burdakin asked him. "That's what I've been doing, and that's where I'm at," responded the man, who was going to keep his salary and job for life. "It doesn't take many people like that," Burdakin adds, "to take the profit out of ten people working hard." His experiences with Penn Central reinforced his priority at Grand Trunk to hire honest people who would tell him the truth, "even when it hurt." Upon hearing those truths, he made it a point to never rant and rave or play the blame game.

Toward the end of Burdakin's railroading career at Grand Trunk, J. Maurice LeClair, a doctor from eastern Ontario with political connections, replaced Robert A. Bandeen as head of Canadian National (CN) in 1982. (Remember: CN was owned by the government.) LeClair admitted he didn't know anything about railroads, but that didn't stop him from announcing early on, in an interview with *Canadian Business* magazine, how he wanted to "slim down" CN and get rid of a lot of workers. The approach surprised the railroad's employees and caused head-shaking among the company's vice presidents, who knew such a sensitive issue should be discussed with labor and managers before being leaked to Canada's major business magazine. LeClair had earlier invited Burdakin to share any constructive criticism with him. So Burdakin wrote LeClair a two-page letter, telling him—in a nice way—it was a bad idea to "brag" about laying off people in a magazine article. The letter led to an invitation to lunch with LeClair in Montreal. Burdakin again cautioned LeClair about the problems he was creating with such talk. "It wasn't a nice conversation," Burdakin recalls.

He says he was leaving LeClair's office when Rosemary Dunnville, one of LeClair's two secretaries, got up, came around her desk, and kissed Burdakin on the cheek, saying he was the only person to tell LeClair what he needed to hear and what no one else dared tell him.

That kiss would be the only "reward" Burdakin would receive. LeClair— apparently apprehensive about Burdakin's aspirations—named Gerry Maas as president of Grand Trunk and "promoted" Burdakin to vice chairman of the Grand Trunk Corporation, where Burdakin would work on unfinished business, such as a minor lawsuit involving Penn Central. Burdakin says LeClair told him at the time that "you have to remember you were after my job." Nothing, Burdakin says, could have been further from the truth.

"I only had three years left before I would be at the mandatory retirement age of sixty-five," he says. "It would have taken three years before I could even see and memorize everywhere Canadian National tracks ran. And it also would have taken at least three years before CN officers would have confidence in me and know I wouldn't knife them in the back. The simple fact is that I was removed as president of Grand Trunk. It was a polite way of being fired."

John Burdakin retired in 1987, his integrity intact. He was invited to serve on Grand Trunk Western's Board of Directors, but for one year rather than the five years that had been general practice. It was not the ending Burdakin would have written to what had been, up until then, a stellar career in railroad management. But it was the ending he got, and it was one he eventually made his peace with. He left knowing, too, he had done his best and had always tried to do the right thing.

TAKEAWAYS

- Don't tell people you're retiring unless you are ready to lose authority—or be ignored.
- Don't pick your successor. Leave that to someone else.
- Make your points, but avoid pushing arguments to the point you make enemies.
- Don't leave your job until you have another one.

Men work to clear the wreckage of two trains near Coshocton, Ohio, on September 11, 1950. The accident killed thirty-three people, many of them National Guard soldiers. John Burdakin's experience managing the cleanup for the Pennsylvania Railroad forged his lifelong commitment to railroad safety. (Photo courtesy of Coshocton Fire Department)

CHAPTER 3

WHEN YOU SEE A PROBLEM,

FIND SOLUTIONS

John Burdakin's emphasis on safety and railroad rules began early in his career when he was assistant track supervisor for the Pennsylvania Railroad (PRR) in Coshocton, Ohio. He'd been left in charge while his boss was on vacation, a situation Burdakin took as "a major vote of confidence: being left in charge of 'his' railroad." His phone rang at 6:35 a.m. on September 11, 1950. A PRR passenger train, speeding along in heavy fog, had rear-ended a stopped troop train carrying National Guard soldiers from northeastern Pennsylvania. Thirty-two people were dead; another seriously injured soldier died in the hospital the following day.

Burdakin arrived at the scene to find two locomotives on their sides, one sideways on the track, coach cars completely destroyed, cars compressed with bodies inside. "It was a horrible sight, one I'll never forget," he says. He was especially worried about Doug Hasbrook, a recent college graduate who'd just started as a junior engineer with PRR and who was on the National Guard train. Before Doug left, Burdakin told him to ride with the crew in the last car on the train and, if the train stopped for any unexplained reason, to get off with the crew so he could report what he saw. To this day, Burdakin recalls the "joy and relief" he felt when he was surveying the wreckage and heard Doug call his name. Doug had followed Burdakin's instructions and gotten off the troop train when it stopped. Doug and the crew found that an air hose had uncoupled, causing the train's brakes to set. They'd heard the approaching passenger train's whistle and assumed it would see the yellow caution signal and stop. It didn't. The safety instructions Burdakin had given Doug, almost in passing, likely saved Doug's life. Doug was devastated by the experience and found he couldn't be around train tracks and moving trains any longer without suffering great anxiety. He resigned within a month.

Burdakin, while shaken by the experience, continued in the business but with an acute awareness of how dangerous railroading can be and with a lifetime commitment to making the work as safe as possible. "To be at the scene, involved in such a major disaster, as well as being responsible for railroad property and restoring train operations—well, it has forced many hours of reflection," Burdakin says.

When Burdakin was the assistant trainmaster in Cincinnati with the Pennsylvania Railroad, from 1960 to 1961, his superiors recommended he take a leave of absence and, at the request of Congress, run the government-owned Panama Railroad for one year, an assignment later extended to fifteen months. Early on, Burdakin was informed that the Panama Railroad's morning northbound train hadn't followed the correct procedure in moving to the siding to let the southbound train pass. "I couldn't have that," Burdakin recalls. "It could have been a head-on collision. Obviously, it was a major mistake, and I could not let it pass. I took the engineer out of service and then held an investigation and trial, resulting in a thirty-day suspension for the engineer. I didn't make a big deal of it. Just made the point that I would not ignore failure to obey the operating rules. It was the only suspension I had to give in Panama."

Another example of putting safety first came when Burdakin, then a vice president for Penn Central's Lakes Region in Cleveland in 1968, tangled with Alfred E. Perlman, Penn Central's CEO and the former president of the New York Central. Perlman was pushing and deeply interested in "van" trains, an alternative to the "piggyback" trailers on flat cars (TOFC). The concept was called "Flexi-Van" and was based on the fact that shipping a van, or a container, instead of a full trailer would eliminate weight and wind resistance. Thus, van trains could save fuel while achieving higher track speeds.[1] The increased speed helped market the service. Flexi-Van containers also required less vertical clearance than a highway trailer or a flat car, thus allowing intermodal operations on lines where overpasses, tunnels, and other infrastructure components could not accommodate TOFC equipment.

One day, Burdakin was riding in a locomotive across his territory, from Cleveland to Buffalo. He noticed the engineer was not reducing the locomotive's speed when signals were showing a yellow caution light, which meant the train should be approaching the next signal prepared to stop. Burdakin asked the engineer why he wasn't slowing the train, as required by operating rules. He learned the Penn Central engineers had been instructed to ignore the rule in order to meet the van trains' schedules.

"What do you do in a fog?" Burdakin asked.

"You pray," the engineer replied.

Burdakin couldn't let the matter rest. He talked to railroad test and signal engineers in Cleveland. He learned the van trains could not stop as quickly as standard rolling stock because they were traveling faster. Everyone he talked to knew about the difficulty in stopping, but no one was doing anything. Burdakin says he spent a couple of sleepless nights envisioning collisions. "This was along Lake Erie, with lots of storms, fog, and snow," Burdakin recalls. "With my luck, this was an accident waiting to happen." And so Burdakin ordered a speed restriction in his territory on the CEO's favorite van trains. No one contradicted that order because, he says, "They knew I was right."

SIMILAR ISSUES AT GRAND TRUNK WESTERN

When Burdakin was put in charge of the Grand Trunk Western Railroad (GTW) in 1971, he found a demoralized workplace with deep labor-management issues and little leadership. He needed a way to get the two sides talking and working together. Improving railroad safety was the avenue.

"In the railroad business, you have to realize you're moving big, heavy pieces of machinery, and if you don't handle them right, it is possible to develop big problems," Burdakin says. "Safety is the first responsibility of every railroad employee. You have to have rules. If you follow them, many tragic accidents can be avoided. The rules are the result of many years of railroad experience. I have seen many close calls, injuries, even deaths, which would have or could have been avoided if the Safety Rule Book had been followed.

"Somehow, I had to get that message across to a lot of people. We all have egos, we're all human, and we all want to do it the easy way. We may think the rules are obvious and probably unnecessary." Burdakin came to the Grand Trunk Western from the old Pennsylvania Railroad, which later merged with the New York Central to become Penn Central. The Pennsylvania, he says, had a much more active safety program than either Penn Central or the Grand Trunk.

"When I arrived at Grand Trunk, the first thing foremen were supposed to do every day was to remind employees about 'the rule of the day.' But no concerted effort was being made to impress the importance of safety, even simple things like looking both ways before crossing a rail. I suspect there had never been a discipline case for employees who were observed doing something unsafe. It's not that you want to punish an employee for doing something unsafe—the injury is penalty enough—you just want safety encouraged and rules followed."

"I had to push pretty hard to cut the number of injuries at Grand Trunk," he says. "In my mind, it was all part of running the operation properly. Previous management had not pushed safety. As a vice president I once worked for said, 'Nothing withstands constant pressure, and, if you want proof, look at the Grand Canyon.'"

Part of any effective safety campaign, Burdakin adds, is getting the support of union leadership. While that would seem easy to do, it wasn't, given that some union leaders at the time received, in return for their advice, a share of any financial settlement awarded injured employees. And while there are good business reasons to push safety—cutting the time lost to accidents, avoiding the claims due injured workers—the main reason to push safety is simple: Keeping employees strong and healthy.

"There's no question railroading is a dangerous business," Burdakin says. "You're out there working, both at night and in the daylight, in the rain and in the snow, and it's very easy to get in the wrong place at the wrong time and be badly hurt. A big part of my job was making sure people worked safely. Step one was learning from the mistakes of others. Every employee had a safety book. The book contained lessons learned from accidents in the past—how they occurred and what to do or not do so they wouldn't happen again."

For example, Burdakin was riding the Grand Trunk ferry, which hauled freight cars across Lake Michigan between Muskegon, Michigan, and Milwaukee, Wisconsin. Burdakin asked the captain why he hadn't sounded the ferry's horn when the three hundred–foot ferry was backing away from the dock. The Coast Guard requires that big ships sound a horn to warn smaller boats the big one is going to move. The ferry skipper told Burdakin, "We don't bother with that." Needless to say, that changed, then and there.

Another example of his concern for safety occurred when Burdakin became concerned about the Grand Trunk trains running through East Lansing on the Saturdays the Michigan State University football team played home games. Huge crowds of people were crossing Grand Trunk rails. Burdakin asked why Grand Trunk was moving trains through such a congested area. The answer was that the railroad was there before the football stadium. "Yes, our tracks were there first, but with such crowds crossing our mainline, I needed to eliminate the possibility of a disaster," Burdakin says. He ordered the trains slowed to a crawl before and after games.

The most serious accident during Burdakin's time at Grand Trunk happened in Kalamazoo, Michigan, in 1972, shortly after he had been named the railroad's vice president of operations. Huck Kohl, a locomotive fireman, had hopped off a locomotive to throw a switch so rail cars could be switched to another track. It was dark. The cars ended up on a track where Kohl didn't expect them. He was knocked to the ground and run over. He lost both legs and one arm.

Art Fettig was working in the Grand Trunk's Claims Department and was called to the scene. He took pictures, drew sketches, and buried some of the body parts.

"I'd been in the army as a combat rifleman in Korea and had seen far too much of death and horrors. I'd been wounded myself in combat," Fettig says. "But this was no battlefield, and it seemed so wrong to me what had happened to Huck. . . . It never seemed to get any better. We just kept on killing people at railroad crossings, and our employees kept on getting injured on the job."

The following morning, he decided he'd had it and thought seriously of quitting his job. But his main concern was Huck Kohl.

"I figured if I could get one top executive to talk with Huck, it might give Huck some hope for the future," Fettig recalls. "I prayed that I might find someone in authority who might care enough to do something to see that there would never be such a senseless tragedy again."

Fettig called Burdakin, the railroad's new vice president.

"I was half scared to death because in the twenty-four years I had worked with the railroad, I had never met a railroad vice president," Fettig says.[2]

Burdakin immediately agreed to go with Fettig to the hospital and visit the injured fireman. They talked about railroad safety on that drive. It was the beginning of a beautiful friendship and a fruitful working relationship that had safety at its heart.

"That was forty years ago, but I will never forget the morning I first shook hands with Mr. Burdakin," says Fettig, who is now retired and lives in North Carolina.

Fettig told Burdakin about the rotten attitudes of both management and labor on the railroad. He talked about the homework he'd been doing on human behavior, motivation, and attitudes. He played Burdakin a song he'd written—"What's a Grand Trunk?"—intended to instill pride in the workplace and its "new team."

It took a while, but Burdakin created a job for Fettig—employee communications officer—and turned Fettig loose to create scores of slide shows, pamphlets, and safety programs. Faced with the prospect of safety programs that were boring, Fettig created "Joe No No," an "accident walking around waiting to happen." Joe broke all the safety rules and would get hurt. "Don't be a Joe No-No," safety posters would caution. "We need you on the job."

Fettig would later become a nationally known motivational speaker and safety expert. And it all started with a terrible accident, a handshake, and a railroad executive who listened and then acted.

As for Huck Kohl, the locomotive fireman who'd lost three limbs, after he adjusted to his prostheses, Burdakin found him a job in the Grand Trunk's Superintendent's Office in Battle Creek, Michigan. Kohl later would manage the computer center in the railroad's Detroit headquarters, where he worked until he retired. "It might be one of the finest rehab stories involving a triple amputation case one could find," Fettig says.

DON'T BURN YOUR BRIDGES, AND KEEP
LOOKING FOR OPPORTUNITIES

In 1971, John Burdakin was vice president of operations for Grand Trunk Western and was walking to lunch with his boss, Robert A. Bandeen, when Bandeen asked his advice about a huge wooden bridge on the Duluth, Winnipeg & Pacific (DWP) line between International Falls and Duluth, Minnesota. A year earlier, Canadian National (CN) engineers had recommended that the all-timber bridge, almost a mile long, be replaced with a steel bridge at an estimated cost of $43 million in 1970. "I said I had never been to Duluth, and I admitted to my complete ignorance, but I had to agree that was a lot of money," Burdakin recalls. "Bandeen then asked what I would do. I said I'd get a second opinion. 'How do I do that?' was his retort." Burdakin took care of it, recommending a "real solid" bridge engineer he had worked with at the Pennsylvania Railroad. The engineer, who had recently retired and been widowed, inspected every timber on the bridge, noting the ones that needed to be replaced. DWP crews did the repair work for less than $80,000.

The solution for the bridge brought up another "opportunity": how to reroute traffic while the bridge was under repair. Burdakin saw that another, smaller railroad—the Duluth, Missabe and Iron Range Railroad (DM&IR), owned by U.S. Steel—was nearby. He negotiated trackage rights for about ten miles of that line and built a one thousand–foot connection between the DWP and DM&IR tracks.[3] It turned out that CN/DWP trains, by using the trackage rights, could avoid going through downtown Duluth entirely. The new route allowed trains to move directly into yards in Superior, Wisconsin, where they would connect with other carriers. The creative solution freed land in downtown Duluth to extend Interstate 35 through the city, eventually netting the railroad millions of dollars, which it plowed into a new office, a new engine house, and a new car repair facility in Wisconsin. The advantages to Grand Trunk and DWP were enormous. "You don't often receive support from all parties involved," Burdakin says. But that was the case in this instance, with the city of Duluth, the Minnesota Highway Department, the Federal Highway Administration, two railroads, and labor all in favor.

The plan, however, could not have endeared Burdakin to CN engineers, who could have spotted such a solution years ago. By not having to build a new steel bridge, Canadian National saved $43 million immediately and $8 million to $10 million in operating expenses annually.

"I regret I did not order a study to determine the actual operating savings and the additional revenue to Canadian National from our added traffic," Burdakin says. "Of course, I strengthened and rebuilt the thousand feet of new track and added two remote-controlled switches. I did not order the actual savings study, though. I was afraid I had embarrassed the CN engineers enough."

Another opportunity presented itself in 1971. The railroad wanted to get out of the commuter business between Pontiac and Detroit, a major cash drain on the railroad. During this period of time, the railroad industry was still highly regulated by the Interstate Commerce Commission (ICC). The nature of regulation in this case would not allow railroads to abandon service that affected the "public interest." This was especially true of passenger service, which was extremely difficult to abandon. If Burdakin was going to be able to get out of the passenger service, he was going to have to find a creative solution. It turned out the Southeastern Michigan Transportation Authority wanted to operate the commuter business but had very little cash to buy it. So Burdakin negotiated a deal wherein the Authority reimbursed Grand Trunk one-third of the railroad's commuter losses each year for a three-year period. In turn, Grand Trunk agreed to sell the Authority one-third of the commuter equipment and facilities each year for three years. The Authority also took over the commuter route's ticketing and operations. Patience was rewarded. At the end of three years, Grand Trunk was out of the commuter business. The agreement covered the GTW's losses and saved the railroad a bundle by avoiding years of costly hearings before the ICC.

"An accounting manager criticized me for not getting out of the commuter business [sooner] and getting it sold all at once," Burdakin says. "But I figured it was better to get a third of the money over three years rather than pin my hopes on the ICC rendering a favorable decision."

Put Problems in Perspective

Another story, which demonstrated the need for a sense of humor, occurred during the Reagan administration when Elizabeth Dole was the U.S. Secretary of Transportation (1983–1987). Two railroads—the CSX System and the Norfolk Southern Railway (NS)—were interested in acquiring all or part of Conrail.[4] The Reagan administration was strongly in favor of putting Conrail on a self-sustaining basis rather than becoming a black hole of unending subsidies. CSX was interested in splitting up Conrail, while the NS was interested in acquiring Conrail.[5] Secretary Dole supported the case of the NS. Burdakin and Grand Trunk opposed the acquisition of Conrail by either railroad on the basis of competitive equity.

Burdakin and Washington, D.C., attorney Basil Cole made their case to staffers at the Federal Railroad Administration and to other transportation officials, including Secretary Dole. The GTW estimated that approximately 68,000 revenue carloads were at risk of diversion to a NS-Conrail combination.[6] Part of the objection by the GTW was based on the practice of merged railroads closing gateways or interchange points to other carriers—thereby avoiding the need to share revenue with connecting carriers.[7] For a regional railroad like the Grand Trunk, which depended on connecting traffic, competing with ever-larger systems could be a disaster.

Burdakin didn't return to his office in Detroit until around 11 A.M. the next day. That's when he learned twenty-three federal railroad inspectors "were inspecting my little railroad." Burdakin chalked it up to the Grand Trunk not supporting the Federal Railroad Administration and Dole's decision to back the Norfolk Southern's bid for Conrail. "She was rattling my cage with that many inspectors on our thousand-plus miles of track. She was sending me a message," Burdakin says. "So I called her up and thanked her because she was doing my job—that is, making sure the Grand Trunk was running all right. I told her I needed all the help I could get." That approach, rather than anger and angst, worked. The federal inspectors were quietly withdrawn, and, as far as Burdakin knows, they found nothing wrong during the surprise inspection blitz.

TAKEAWAYS

- John Burdakin recognized the pervasive need for rules in the railroad industry. Some people might question all the rules in railroading. They're the people who haven't stood on an embankment on a foggy morning and seen devastation and death. For good railway managers, safety is ingrained, and the need to follow operating rules is a religion. "They're there for a reason. If you don't like a rule, work on getting it changed," Burdakin says. "Don't ignore the rule just because it appears, to you, to be generally unnecessary or time-consuming."
- Providing a safe environment for workers requires a human element as well as strict adherence to rules.
- When problem-solving, be persistent, on the one hand, and creative, on the other. Recognize that solving one problem will often lead to another—and another.

John H. Burdakin, president of the Grand Trunk Western Railroad, 1976. (Photo from John H. Burdakin collection)

CHAPTER 4

YOU WON'T WIN THEM ALL

REALIZING YOU CAN'T WIN EVERY BATTLE, WHILE SOBERING, MAY BE the most important of John Burdakin's management principles. As a manager, you win some, but you also lose some—even when you're right. How managers deal with such setbacks can often determine their future.

Perhaps the most challenging setback Burdakin experienced came in 1961 when he was manager of transportation engineering at the Pennsylvania Railroad's (PRR) corporate headquarters in Philadelphia. He had spent months working on two projects—a test of weigh-in-motion scales and a test to expand the PRR's radio communications.

The weigh-in-motion scales were a new technology that promised to weigh, with adequate accuracy, bulk commodities like coal or iron ore. Rather than having to separate each freight car from a train and weigh it individually, the cars could be dragged slowly across the scales, and a close-to-actual weight determined much more quickly. Burdakin worked with the developer and came up with a contract that would test the technology on four hundred feet of new, 140-pound welded rail that the railroad would pay to install. If the scales didn't meet specified standards of accuracy, the developer would remove them at his expense. The PRR's legal department had approved the contract.

The second project called for testing radio equipment to improve communication between railroad employees up and down the Delmarva Peninsula, from Wilmington, Delaware, to Cape Charles, Virginia. Communication, at the time, was handled via a telephone line strung alongside the track, a system that had been put in place as an experiment ten years earlier. The system was repaired and maintained by workers from the engine house in Wilmington. The annual repair charges, Burdakin found, totaled more than the cost of extending the new radios to all operations.

To proceed, both projects required only a signature from someone at the vice president's level at the PRR. The folders landed on the desk of Park Roeper, who had been recently promoted to assistant vice president of operations for the Eastern Region. He called Burdakin in to talk about the projects. The meeting lasted ten minutes, during which Roeper summarily rejected both projects. Roeper said the Baltimore & Ohio Railroad (B&O) was experimenting with the weigh-in-motion scales and that the PRR would let them do the testing. Roeper also said he didn't believe the engine house in Wilmington was actually spending as many man-hours and as much money as it claimed keeping the telephone communications line and the locomotives working on the Delmarva Peninsula.

A discouraged Burdakin took the two project folders back to his office, threw them on his desk, and walked the streets of Philadelphia for three hours, considering whether he should quit his job. "Here the mighty PRR, the biggest railroad in the country, was not going to experiment with weigh-in-motion scales but rather let the mighty, but small, B&O experiment with them," Burdakin says. "And no attempt was going to be made to verify if the engine house in Wilmington was accurately charging for repairs to the communications system.

"If this is what managing transportation on the PRR was going to be like, why am I here, why don't I quit? There's no way this railroad can keep the respect it's earned over the years, as 'the standard' railroad of the world, with this kind of leadership. The PRR couldn't maintain solvency with that kind of thinking," he concluded.

"If it hadn't been for having three boys and a wife at home, I'd have quit that day. It became evident later on, of course, that the old PRR wasn't going to survive, that it had deep, deep financial problems. The handwriting was on the wall."

Burdakin swallowed his disappointment and, after the PRR and New York Central merged to become Penn Central, he was named vice president and general manager for Penn Central's Lakes Region in 1968. It was his self-control and forbearance—along with his managerial skills—that put him where he needed to be to become vice president of operations at Grand Trunk Western (GTW) in 1971 and, shortly afterward, its president.

ATTEMPTS TO INTRODUCE INDUSTRY-WIDE TECHNOLOGY

Burdakin, as president of the Grand Trunk Western Railroad in the 1970s, began instituting Automatic Car Identification (ACI) on GTW freight cars. He had appeared before the Association of American Railroads' Board of Directors and convinced its members to put the multicolored metal labels on railcars. Trackside scanners would read the labels and report where the railcar was, which railroad owned the car, and which direction it was going. The new technology—the precursor of today's ubiquitous bar codes—promised to increase efficiency and automate a paperwork process that was then handled by hundreds of clerks.[1] At the same time this was happening, the union representing railroad clerks was negotiating a national contract—promising significant labor strife, if not a nationwide strike, in response to ACI.

"I was not involved in those negotiations," Burdakin says. "However, I am confident ACI was the big issue, not wages." In the end, a nationwide strike was avoided when a major western railroad ordered three hundred new cars, stipulating no labels. This broke the back of the voluntary initiative that all cars be labeled and delayed the introduction of the new technology.

There were at least two challenges to the implementation of the ACI program. First, in order for the system to have any value, it would need to label

43

every car for every railroad—a difficult task for a voluntary initiative. The second problem was that the system couldn't produce an acceptable level of accuracy. When the labels got dirty, trackside scanners couldn't read them, and the experiment was abandoned in the late 1970s.

Twenty years later, a more functionally effective form of the new technology was universally established and approved, under the guise of the Association of American Railroads, with savings enjoyed.[2] "One of my major regrets," Burdakin says, "is that I could not convince the industry to adopt the technology earlier, but I am proud that the Grand Trunk was one of the early, major advocates of the concept."

CHANGING LABOR LAWS

In another example, Burdakin—and railroad executives throughout the country—were trying to remove the requirement that a fireman be aboard every locomotive. Firemen at one time tended to the fuel and combustion needs on coal- and oil-fired steam locomotives, a job no longer needed on diesel locomotives, but jobs the union was fighting to preserve. Burdakin entered into the time-consuming legal process of opening the union contract and posting new operating rules to remove firemen from locomotives on the Central Vermont Railway, owned by Grand Trunk/Canadian National. The Central Vermont was a small railroad, and if a strike was called, Burdakin figured, it wouldn't significantly hurt Canadian National (CN) or Grand Trunk operations. It was a good chance to test the waters. Burdakin's bosses at Canadian National, sensing a breakthrough, urged him onward. Until, that is, the union announced it was prepared to picket CN's corporate headquarters—and the railroad president's home—in Montreal if the company proceeded with the program. The bloom immediately fell off that reformist rose, and Burdakin was told to drop the effort. Years later, of course, firemen were removed from all diesel locomotives.

DOOMED BY HIS OWN SUCCESS

After the Staggers Act (1980), a new series of railroad mergers and acquisitions began to reconcile the wounded rail network from the 1970s. The management of GTW realized the railroad needed to get larger if it was going to survive. GTW was primarily an originating carrier, serving the automotive industry in the Detroit area. It didn't control both the origin and destination of most of its traffic. Thus, it always had to share the revenue with a connecting carrier. It needed to expand so it had more control over "local" traffic, that is, shipments where it controlled both origin and destination.

The Chicago, Milwaukee, St. Paul & Pacific Railroad (Milwaukee Road) entered bankruptcy in 1977 and, over the years, had been pared from a transcontinental system to a Midwest regional railroad of about 3,100 miles. The core of the pared-down Milwaukee was Kansas City, Chicago, and Minneapolis/St. Paul with access to Duluth, Minnesota, over trackage rights. Acquisition of the Milwaukee would give GTW long-haul capabilities involving Detroit, Chicago, Kansas City, and Minneapolis/St. Paul. Perhaps more important, the acquisition would provide access to Duluth, which would unite the GTW with the Duluth, Winnipeg & Pacific (DWP) and ultimately the CN over Fort Frances, Ontario/International Falls, Minnesota. Such a routing would provide efficient through train movement from and to western Canada and the eastern United States.

One problem was that the GTW was in the process of digesting the recently acquired DT&I.[3] There were a couple of other problems. The physical condition of the Milwaukee had continued to deteriorate following its fall into bankruptcy in 1977, and the GTW did not have any cash available to acquire the property, let alone make improvements. Meanwhile, the CN had made it clear that its U.S. subsidiaries—that is, GTW, DWP and CV—had to stand on their own.[4] The good news was, up to this point, no other railroad was interested in the Milwaukee, leaving the field clear for Burdakin.[5] He developed a two-part plan. At merger, the GTW would absorb the Milwaukee's debt. In addition, the GTW would enter into a Voluntary Coordination Agreement (VCA) that involved routing CN traffic over DWP onto the Milwaukee. The

VCA was intended to inject revenue into the Milwaukee so that it could begin to revitalize itself.[6] Also, it was not subject to ICC approval and could be effective immediately.

It is not clear, but entirely possible, that John Burdakin invented the VCA. At a minimum, it was a unique approach to the objective of allowing the GTW to acquire the Milwaukee. By 1982, it had become apparent that it was working. On March 31, 1983, the trustee of the Milwaukee submitted a plan to allow the reenergized Milwaukee to emerge from bankruptcy and become a subsidiary of the Grand Trunk Corporation.[7] There were just a couple of problems. The cars that were diverted to the Milwaukee were not new business, but traffic that had been enjoyed by other connecting carriers, for example, the Chicago & North Western and the Soo Line railroads. Noticing a drop in their own traffic, they quickly realized that, in the hands of the GTW, the Milwaukee was suddenly a valuable property. They also realized that the GTW was trying to make the acquisition with little or no cash. They quickly began a bidding war that reached $500 million (Soo) and $700 million (C&NW). After having made the Milwaukee healthy, the Grand Trunk was left at the altar. The Soo eventually acquired the Milwaukee in February 1985 for approximately $500 million. The difference in the proposals with the C&NW was that the Soo did not plan substantial abandonment of Milwaukee lines.[8] In the words of Byron Olsen, Soo's vice president and general counsel at the time, "Everyone who benefited from the Milwaukee Road sale owes a debt of gratitude to Grand Trunk."[9]

TAKEAWAYS

- Remember the principle of looking at a problem and striving for a solution until it's found. Win or lose, it feeds your creativity.
- Persevere. Change is difficult. In the railroad industry, it may be damn near impossible.
- Be a visionary. Don't think outside the box—think outside the boxcar.

John Burdakin (*right*) celebrates a new Grand Trunk Western radio tower, one of the first capital improvements he pursued after becoming GTW president in 1974. (Photo courtesy of Michigan Railroad History Museum)

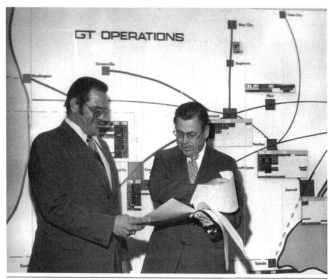

John H. Burdakin (*right*) goes over Grand Trunk Western operations with Jim DiBona (*left*) in 1977. (Photo courtesy of Michigan Railroad History Museum)

CHAPTER 5

HIRE GOOD PEOPLE

John Burdakin allows he did have a knack for assessing talent and attracting good people to work for him. Burdakin says he hired the best, most experienced people he could—sometimes convincing people who were unhappy at other, bigger railroads to come work for the smaller Grand Trunk. He couldn't offer them as much money, but he offered them a compelling challenge: You'll be left alone to manage to the best of your ability. In short, he empowered his managers. He gave them the same freedom—and expectations—he enjoyed with his boss and mentor, Canadian National's president, Robert A. Bandeen.

"I could do anything I wanted to do if I kept Bandeen informed," he says. "But if Bandeen or others read about something in the newspaper, something I'd neglected to tell Bandeen about, then I'd have to do a lot of explaining." Burdakin says he was always available to his managers and superiors, answering their questions and making decisions when needed. "I didn't hesitate to pat people on the back," he adds. "But I didn't micromanage people. I knew I couldn't micromanage as well from headquarters as they could manage directly on-site."

HIRING PASSIONATE PEOPLE

Five of the exceptional hires he made at Grand Trunk, he says, were Basil Cole, Bill Glavin, Bob Adams, James Elliott, and Art Fettig. Burdakin says he talked Cole, the attorney who'd handled the Penn Central bankruptcy, out of retiring to lobby and represent Grand Trunk's interests in Washington, D.C. Burdakin recognized he needed Cole—"the most respected transportation lawyer in Washington"—and found a way to pay him by sharing his costs with the Pittsburgh and Lake Erie Railroad. Cole also was very effective, Burdakin says, in presenting cases before the Interstate Commerce Commission (ICC) in the Grand Trunk purchase of the Detroit & Toledo Shore Line Railway and the Detroit, Toledo and Ironton Railroad. The Grand Trunk, Burdakin says, was fortunate to have Cole as its counsel.

Burdakin hired Elliott to run Grand Trunk's ferry boats on Lake Michigan, where he was a "stabilizing influence." Elliott had been a successful businessman before World War II selling carpeting, and after the war selling hospital and factory food services. He loved the Great Lakes, had a captain's license, and owned a fifty-six-foot yacht. It was a small step from that boat to Grand Trunk ferries. Elliott also supplied a number of truisms about business that Burdakin loved: "Business without a profit is no business." "Little hogs get bigger; big hogs get slaughtered."

Burdakin hired both Glavin and Adams away from the bigger, but troubled, Penn Central—Glavin as chief engineer for Grand Trunk and Adams as its superintendent of transportation. He had worked with both men at the Pennsylvania Railroad and knew they were excellent managers. Both chose to work for him, probably for less money than they'd been earning at Penn Central, because Burdakin and Grand Trunk offered a more civil, honest workplace.

Adams, at the time of his hire, was general manager for Penn Central's New York Region, responsible for the comings and goings of a thousand trains a day. "Talk about a manager!" Burdakin says of Adams. Burdakin says he had to stretch to hire Adams and offered him a salary only $1,000 less than he himself was making. "I don't know how much money Bob gave up to come out west to Detroit and work with me again," Burdakin says, "but it was considerable."

Burdakin plucked Fettig out of relative obscurity when Fettig was a Grand Trunk claims agent, and created a job for him as employee communications officer. Fettig would become nationally known for his safety and employee communications programs and for his skills as a public speaker.

"I believe that Mr. Burdakin managed most everyone under his leadership in the way he found worked best for them," Fettig says. "He looked at the job to be done and tried to put the right person in that spot where he or she would have the best chance of success. And then he did everything he could to help that person succeed. I believe he relished the success of others."

LEARNING WHAT NOT TO DO

After finding and hiring good people, of course, a good manager must work at keeping them, treating them well, and constantly challenging them. Burdakin says he saw managers doing the exact opposite of that during his days with the Pennsylvania Railroad, particularly after its merger with the New York Central.[1] Burdakin, who was put in charge of Penn Central's Lakes Region, based in Cleveland, reported to Ed Claypool, who'd come from the New York Central. Each day, transportation managers along the line talked by phone about the previous day and the upcoming one. For some reason, Burdakin says, he was late getting to one of those morning meetings. "I came into the room, and Ed Claypool was chastising my movement people for being 'dumb, ignorant, not knowing what they're doing'—all the negatives a person could think of. This was coming in over a loudspeaker. I listened for a while and then jumped in, saying I didn't appreciate the way this conversation was going. And if anyone had a problem with my movement people, I would appreciate it if they would talk to me so I could correct any deficiency. I said I knew enough about what was going on that I didn't believe my people were dumb or stupid or laying down on the job."

Five minutes after the meeting ended, Burdakin's phone rang in his office. It was Ed Claypool—a very upset Ed Claypool. Burdakin was upset, too. The conversation "got louder and louder," Burdakin says. "Ed finally said he was going to come out to Cleveland and punch me in the nose. I told him he didn't need to do that. He made more money than I did. If he wanted to punch me in the nose, I'd come to his office whenever he said." Though Claypool didn't take him up on the offer, Burdakin says that was the way New York Central managed its transportation offices and employees.

"It's not my way of doing things," Burdakin says. "I had never talked to anyone the way Ed Claypool was talking to my people. I thought, at the time, that's real nice—two vice presidents of a railroad getting into a boxing match. I was upset that any officer, particularly a vice president, would talk to any employee like that. Calling people names is not management."

TAKEAWAYS

- Hire the people who excite you.
- Demand feedback—as much as you need.
- You've got enough to do—avoid micromanagement. Don't be a "hover manager."
- Working for a small railroad is more fun than working for a big one.

John Burdakin and Jean Campbell Moulton on their wedding day, October 2, 1948, with Jean's parents, Jane and George Moulton (*left*), and John's parents, Martha and Richard Burdakin (*right*). The wedding was at the home of Jean's parents in Milton, Massachusetts. (Photo from John H. Burdakin collection)

Jean and John Burdakin sit on the porch of their first home in Havre de Grace, Maryland. (Photo from John H. Burdakin collection)

CHAPTER 6

CHOOSE CAREFULLY
WHOM YOU MARRY

CAREFULLY SELECTING ONE'S SPOUSE MIGHT SEEM LIKE UNUSUAL advice to find in a management book, but John Burdakin believes no decision has a greater impact on your life than whom you marry. "Ninety percent of your happiness—or unhappiness—stems from that decision," Burdakin says. "Your choice not only ensures a happy home, but it also can become a major factor in helping your career."

John Howard Burdakin and Jean Campbell Moulton were married in 1948 and had sixty-three happy years together before Jean died in 2012. Jean was a graduate of Radcliffe College, where she was president of her senior class. "She could talk to anyone, could talk intelligently and sympathetically on about any subject, and could make everyone feel welcomed," Burdakin says of his wife.

When Canadian National would have its big corporate dinners in Montreal in the 1970s and 1980s, the president and CEO, Robert A. Bandeen, would always seat Jean to his right. She said it was because she was married to the only American officer in the Canadian corporation, so Bandeen could pick her and the Canadian vice presidents and their spouses wouldn't feel slighted. But Bandeen's wife, Mona, later said no, that wasn't it. He just enjoyed talking to Jean.

Over the years, the Burdakins moved sixteen times because of John's career, a challenge that Jean handled with grace and aplomb—and never a complaint, her husband says. She dealt with movers, lost items, and new schools for the three Burdakin sons, making friends and putting people at ease wherever she lived. Her motto—"Bloom where you're planted"— "describes her exactly," Burdakin says.

John and Jean met right after World War II, when John had returned to MIT for his senior year. He'd just been discharged from the army as a first lieutenant and was thinking it might be time to consider getting married. He'd had a girlfriend in high school and had dated a nurse while in the army, but neither was a serious romance.

"Here I was, getting older, with no serious girlfriend," Burdakin says.

He had worked hard his first three years at MIT, studying every night. He decided, as a senior, he could take Saturday nights off and do some socializing. A fraternity brother named Bob had been dating Jean Moulton for three years but said she'd finally told him "there was no chemistry." Bob offered to introduce Burdakin to her, thinking maybe they'd hit it off.

He made the introduction. Burdakin liked Jean but didn't call her for a date, thinking perhaps Bob wasn't serious about bowing out. Two weeks later, however, Jean called John, inviting him on a church sleigh ride. She showed up with two blankets rather than one. He got the message, thinking, "This is going to take some time. But, for this, I'll gladly wait." Burdakin says he knew almost immediately that Jean was the woman he wanted to marry. He was heartened, too, in that "she chose me." The two dated for a year after they graduated. Jean worked and lived with her parents in Milton, Massachusetts, and John started his career in New York City with the Pennsylvania Railroad. They were married October 2, 1948.

Jean wrote, in "My Life: Stories for My Children,"[1] that she and John would have married earlier, "but I had promised my parents that if they would agree to let me go to my choice of college, Radcliffe, rather than their choice for me, Bridgewater Normal School, I would work for one year after graduation. I worked as assistant to the Registrar at Radcliffe—a promise kept."

Burdakin says the only argument he and Jean ever had was on their wedding night, about whose brand of toothpaste they would share. That argument was soon settled, he says, smiling at the memory, adding, "She was the perfect wife for me."

TAKEAWAYS

- Deciding whom you marry is one of the most important decisions you will make in your life. Choose carefully.
- Consider the impact on spouses and families in making management decisions.
- As in hiring, marry a person you respect and who excites you.

John Burdakin's parents, Martha and Richard. (Photo from John H. Burdakin collection)

John Burdakin delivering newspapers as a teenager. (Photo from John H. Burdakin collection)

John Burdakin, high school graduation photo. (Photo from John H. Burdakin collection)

Second Lieutenant John Burdakin, U.S. Army, World War II. (Photo from John H. Burdakin collection)

John Burdakin with his great-grandson, Evan Privett, 2014. (Photo courtesy of Julie and Brian Privett)

CHAPTER 7

ENJOY YOUR WORK

AND WORK HARD

PERHAPS THE NEED TO WORK HARD GOES WITHOUT SAYING FOR ANY-
one ambitious enough to want a career in management. From the days John
Burdakin had a newspaper route during the Great Depression, to the days
he was a top railway executive responsible for thousands of jobs, he always
worked hard. "I never felt like I had to 'back up' to the pay window," Burdakin says. "No one could ever say I didn't earn my way. That's the way I was
raised. I had a job, from age twelve on, until I retired."

THE IMPORTANCE OF FAMILY

When money was tight during the Depression, Burdakin saw his mother,
Martha, rise early every Tuesday morning to bake dozens of cookies to sell
at the Woman's Educational and Industrial Union across from the Boston

Commons. Normally, she'd "only" bake thirty to thirty-five dozen cookies a week—sugar, butterscotch, chocolate, and gingersnaps—that people would buy to take home. During the Christmas season, though, she'd bake ninety dozen cookies a week. It was a job she did for more than thirty years—her financial contribution to the family.

Burdakin's father, L. Richard Burdakin, graduated from the Dean Academy, a private high school in Franklin, Massachusetts. Richard's father (Burdakin's grandfather and namesake) was registrar of deeds in Norfolk County, a publicly prominent job he held for many years. Richard's mother raised her son, whom she called Leslie, his first name, the way she thought a "proper Bostonian" should be raised—including the long blond curls he had until he was six years old.

Leslie dropped that name—which he loathed—as soon as he graduated from prep school and thereafter went by the name L. Richard, or "Dick," as he preferred to be called. He headed west, working for a year in the Yellowstone area of Wyoming. He was offered a job breaking horses for Buffalo Bill's Wild West Show but opted instead to return to Boston, where he took a job riding around New England on a motorcycle, checking the condition of utility lines.

One day in 1911, when Dick was working near Hanover, New Hampshire, his motorcycle skidded on gravel and crashed, landing on his leg. The local doctor wanted to amputate the leg, but Dick's father said to wait until the Burdakin family doctor could arrive. The family doctor brought silver wire with him and wired Dick's kneecap in place, saving the leg. Dick returned to Massachusetts to recover and rehab his knee. During that time, he met his sister Lillian's roommate from boarding school, Martha Gertrude Rogers, whom he would later marry.

Dick and Martha made their home in Wollaston, Massachusetts, where Dick was a salesperson for a boiler manufacturing company until it went out of business in 1929, soon after the Great Depression started. After that, he worked as a handyman, taking any job he could find. Dick and Martha had three children. Eleanor was born first, then Dorothy, and then, on August 11, 1922, John Howard Burdakin.

Eleanor, who always loved animals, bred and raised guinea pigs in the family's basement when she was a teenager, selling them to a Boston hospital for use in research. John remembers the day his sister learned her guinea pigs had a disease and that the hospital would no longer accept them. In tears, she drowned each of her beloved guinea pigs in the basement sink. His mother told him not to go downstairs.

It was a tough life lesson, but Burdakin's mother insisted her children see "what goes on in the world." She was the girl, after all, who had disguised herself as a young man so she could get into a burlesque house in Boston to see what went on inside. She became the mother who insisted her daughters watch an inebriated woman stumble along the street so they could see what happens if you drink too much.

By the time he was nine years old, John Burdakin was traveling on buses and subways to downtown Boston on his own. When John, at age thirteen, had a newspaper route, his mother asked him to contribute twenty-five cents a week toward the family's expenses. In sixth grade, she took him out of school to spend three days with family friends who made their living selling merchandise at fairs. It would be a good learning experience for him, she reasoned. And it was. The young Burdakin slept in a tent and saw "the state fair [at Brockton] from the inside."

Though money was extremely tight in the 1930s, Burdakin's parents found a way to help him buy a fifteen-and-a-half-foot snipe-class sailboat. They provided $75, and he put in $75 from his newspaper route savings. He was responsible for all the boat's expenses after that. Burdakin named the boat *Snooky*, his sister Dot's name for their father. It was anchored off the Wollaston Yacht Club on Wollaston Beach, about four blocks from the Burdakin house. The young Burdakin and a neighbor boy, Bob Mansfield, would race *Snooky* on the weekends in Boston Harbor, right where the oceangoing ships came in.

"It's a wonder we didn't get run over," Burdakin says. "*Snooky* was the best-looking boat. I put a new mahogany deck on her with the help of Mr. Shaw, a ship carpenter who lived across the street from us. She wasn't the fastest boat, though we did get third place in one summer twilight series. But I was master of that boat. I was completely responsible for it. And it kept me off the street."

Burdakin's mother also began telling him, when he was four years old, that he was going to college. When the time came, Burdakin set his sights on West

Point because of the free tuition. He didn't make the cut, primarily because the admissions exam tested applicants on ancient history, which wasn't taught at North Quincy High School, and physics, which Burdakin hadn't yet taken.

Plan B: Burdakin's mother asked Dr. Rockwell, the Burdakins' family doctor—the one who'd earlier saved Dick's leg from amputation and who also ran the MIT dispensary—for help in getting her son into MIT, the prestigious private college in nearby Cambridge. The doctor called MIT's dean of students, who interviewed the young Burdakin and then granted him one of the two remaining slots in the next year's freshman class.

The Burdakin family didn't have money to send a child to college, let alone MIT, but the extended family rallied. His mother's uncle, who ran a bookstore in Brockton, Massachusetts, paid half of Burdakin's tuition. A scholarship covered the other half. An uncle in Philadelphia sent $25 a month for commuting and living expenses to the nephew he'd never met "as long as I stayed in college." Burdakin lived at home to keep costs down. The following year, a lawyer cousin covered the expense of membership in a fraternity, Phi Kappa Sigma, believing college was more than just studying. After depleting his savings, Burdakin borrowed money from MIT to cover his third year's expenses.

It was an opportunity not to be squandered. Burdakin worked and studied hard. He sailed the MIT dinghies, played some "very average" hockey, and ran along the shoreline at night to decompress. Called to duty in World War II at the end of his junior year, he paid off his college debt from his modest salary. He completed his last year at MIT after the war, making use of the GI Bill, graduating with a degree in civil engineering in 1947. It was a good time to graduate, with the economy booming and businesses playing catch-up after the war effort.

STARTING A CAREER

Burdakin wanted a career doing work he would enjoy, where he wouldn't be chained to a desk, and where he could be outdoors part of the time, "regardless of what the money was." In those days, a first job often was with the employer you'd work for all your life. Burdakin approached his decision in the logical, clear-eyed way his family and his education had instilled in him. He investigated three opportunities.

The first offer was with a successful small contractor in southern Connecticut who was building school and college buildings. The contractor, however, had two sons in college. "I was afraid the best I could do would be number three in the company," Burdakin says. The second offer was with Bucyrus Erie, a manufacturer of heavy construction equipment such as cranes, power shovels, backhoes, and other machinery that Burdakin had worked with in the army. The job required training and troubleshooting—which was fine—but also being a salesperson. "I never felt I had much salesmanship, so I backed away," he says.

The third possibility was the Pennsylvania Railroad (PRR), which each year hired fifteen to twenty college graduates in varied disciplines and, if they showed promise, trained them for management roles. Burdakin interviewed with several PRR vice presidents at the railroad's Philadelphia headquarters—where he also would finally meet the uncle who'd helped pay for MIT—and came away impressed by the opportunities.

"They took me out for a little trip around Philadelphia," Burdakin recalls. "All I could see was railroads everywhere. Even though the industry might be in trouble, I couldn't visualize it would be abandoned. I saw how big the company was. I felt there'd be a job there as long as I'd need one. I liked the people running the Engineering Department—their enthusiasm and strength."

Burdakin made his choice, signing on as a junior engineer in PRR's Maintenance of Way Department. His first job was at Penn Station in New York City, which was close enough to Boston that he could continue his courtship of Jean Moulton every other weekend. On the weekends he stayed in New York, he would descend into the tunnels beneath Penn Station on Saturday nights, watching as railroad workers replaced rails.

Burdakin's subsequent career and promotions would mean long hours and a lot of moves for his family. But the frequent transfers, he says, exposed him to many styles of management and all aspects of running a railroad. "I know the frequent moves were hard on my sons, who had to adjust to new schools," Burdakin says. "For me, the benefit was seeing how others motivated people under them and above them. Some of the things I learned may not have necessarily been the things PRR wanted me to learn, but almost all of it was useful and educational."

Burdakin tells a story that illustrates one way an inexperienced, but ambitious, young employee can get noticed. At one point during his early training, railroad employees went from a six-day to a five-day week. Executives still worked a half-day on Saturdays. With all the clerks at home, Burdakin learned how to operate PRR's new office copier. When an executive needed copies made on a Saturday morning, Burdakin was there to help. "They'd recognize me, converse with me, and at least knew my name," he says.

One experience with the Grand Trunk also points out how little patience Burdakin had with managers who were unwilling to work as hard as the job demanded. Burdakin had promoted an older man, who'd been thinking about retiring, to be the superintendent back at Battle Creek, Michigan, the man's original home. A derailment east of Battle Creek closed both main lines. "A railroad cannot make money when standing still," Burdakin says. The superintendent assured Burdakin the track would be cleared by 5 P.M. It wasn't, and Burdakin couldn't reach the superintendent, who'd left work to go square dancing.

"Needless to say, I was not pleased," Burdakin says.

The next morning, a Sunday, the superintendent called Burdakin back.

"You told me you were looking forward to retirement," Burdakin told the man. "How about tomorrow?" The superintendent accepted the offer.

THE IMPORTANCE OF FAMILY

Burdakin's son Dan, writing in his book *Suite Talk: A Guide to Business Excellence*, recalls his father's long hours and hard work.[1] He uses the word "relentless" to describe the lessons learned at home: "No matter what endeavor you might seek, give it your all. Give everything you have.

Outwork your peers and your competition. Whether it was my dad rising to become a legend in the transportation industry, John becoming a doctor of medicine, or David becoming the leader of large manufacturing companies—all were, and still are, relentless."

And while John Burdakin thinks "relentless" might be a bit strong, he totally agrees with the admonition to give a job your all and to outwork the competition.

TAKEAWAYS

- Family legacies can help define your goals and aspirations.
- Hard work not only contributes value to your employer but also to your family.
- Always give a full measure.

John and Jean Burdakin with sons David (*left*) and John Jr. (*right*), Panama Railroad, 1960. (Photo from John H. Burdakin collection)

AN OVERVIEW OF GRAND TRUNK

THIS OVERVIEW OF THE GRAND TRUNK RAILROAD AND THE RAIL-road industry shows John Burdakin at the top of his game, with a firm grasp of the issues railroaders face—national policies, deregulation, competition from trucking—and of the potential offered by making better use of equipment, embracing new technology, and improving productivity and safety. Though a few of the points are dated, most are not. Overall, the article shows the breadth of knowledge and the vision a top-level railroad manager must command.

"THE '80S: NOW EVEN MORE CHALLENGING," BY JOHN H. BURDAKIN, PRESIDENT GRAND TRUNK WESTERN RAILROAD

Just 150 years ago, the running of the first steam locomotive marked the beginning of what would become our complex, nationwide railroad industry. One might assume that through all the intervening years the industry would be stabilized and operating smoothly, efficiently, and effectively. Those of us involved in turning the steel wheel on the steel rail amid today's complexities due to rapid change wish this were true.

Today, the tasks we are facing are greater and more diversified with each passing year. And, looking forward, one can see only an increase and a quickening of activity. The future facing our industry will, or can, result in a stronger, more responsive rail network, provided it is confronted with skill and leadership. The challenge we desired when we first applied for a job is now even greater. Accordingly, the feeling of accomplishment is still strong for those who enjoy railroading, an industry sure to be more fascinating than ever before as the '80s unfold.

Space will not permit a full discussion of the specifics that underlie that statement. But I do want to discuss some of the major challenges that we face. In so doing, we must keep in mind the need for patience and to guard against the frustration engendered by the time required to accomplish specific goals.

THE INTERSTATES: A FATAL BLOW

What about government's involvement in business? Especially, our business? Many encouraging signs have developed that indicate an increasing awareness on the part of our elected officials that railroads no longer can survive under the imposed discriminations of the past.

This focus of attention on our industry by Congress was, of course, motivated by the bankruptcy of Penn Central. The other eastern carriers in a similar plight proved that the problem was greater than one company. In an effort to salvage that situation came the 3R Act, the 4R Act, USRA, and, in April 1976, the beginning of Conrail.

People can point a finger at many causes of Penn Central's bankruptcy—and have. But the basic cause was the failure of the United States to have a comprehensive balanced and integrated transportation policy. The signing of the legislation launching the interstate highway system by

President Eisenhower was, in my opinion, the fatal blow. The formulation of this highway system meant that the railroads in the northeast could no longer compete for transporting manufactured goods, the highest revenue-producing traffic, on hauls up to 500 miles. This tremendous advantage of an almost free, limited interference, high-speed right-of-way was soon followed by legislation for heavier and longer trucks and trailers. The northeast railroads were placed in an impossible competitive position.

The railroad industry can survive and can provide the responsive, efficient transportation system demanded by our economy. To do so, however, it must be in a climate that is equal for all modes. We must develop a national transportation policy based upon our heritage of the free enterprise system. If a specific transportation is required by the nation, be it the movement of people by air, grain by train, ore by water, or package freight by truck, but which cannot support its existence through user charges, government assistance is required and proper. Prime examples are the small regional airport and our light density branch lines. However, discrimination between modes such as that resulting from the essentially free right-of-way for water transportation, or that from permitting truck weights on the road that are known to be in excess of the structural capacity of the pavement, are in sharp contrast to the disadvantage we face in the use of our privately maintained right-of-way. The obvious result: a weakening of the railroad plant and our competitive capability.

SOME ENCOURAGING SIGNS

Events have taken place that are encouraging. First, the two Railroad Reorganization Acts, which were endeavors to tackle the problem from the railroad side. Then came the token waterway user charge legislation, certainly an insignificant step but at least one toward equal treatment. The 55 mph law, although a result of the energy crunch, has had the effect of reducing the destructive impact on our highways and corresponding highway maintenance costs. And now the most recent encouraging sign appears, the Staggers Deregulation Bill. Whatever one's view of this legislation, it is an expression of awareness by Congress of the need to address ills within the rail industry.

Three major railroad legislation packages passed within eight years certainly proves the urgency of the situation and the willingness of Congress to act or react. We are encouraged even though the amount of understanding and support falls far short of addressing the basic problem, unequal treatment of the various modes of transportation.

Now, my plea for a national transportation policy—and former Secretary of Transportation William T. Coleman made the first attempt to formulate it—is based upon two assumptions: First, that the American people want their transportation network to remain as a private enterprise, and second, business without a profit is no business.

We are entering a new era indicated by the recent vote, an era of change toward more conservative policies and reduced involvement by government in the free enterprise system.

During this period I hope to see the turning of the Federal Railroad Administration back to its basic charter—promotion of rail opportunities in response to the needs of the people—and away from its tendency to act as a regulatory oversight organization with no accountability for its decisions. There must be an adequate turnover within that organization's ranks that would allow people with fresh transportation outlooks to contribute and so evolve a more practical representation which is so necessary.

REGIONAL RAILROADS MAY BE SHUT OUT

The Staggers Deregulation Act of 1980 offers great potential for strengthening the rail network. But, as with any step forward, there are new hazards.

This legislation, similar to earlier attempts to assist the industry, is less beneficial to small regional carriers. A major area of concern remains. It is the ability of large existing systems and the even larger systems now proposed by merger to utilize their combined rate and route capabilities to exclude small regional carriers from continuing to participate in the traditional transportation markets.

First is the inherent fear that the new flexibility afforded the larger carriers under the Act will permit them to prey upon small carriers. This is especially true of those carriers, both large and small, who are supported by the taxpayer either through federal or state funds. Reductions in tariffs or failure to increase tariffs at least to match the effects of inflation on the part of such concerns will naturally result in attracting traffic from other roads or modes. The resultant deficiencies in revenues, to be recovered from sources not available to privately owned carriers, will have the opposite effect than that intended by the legislation.

This fact, coupled with the recent apparent change of the Interstate Commerce Commission from its historical position of imposing traffic protective conditions in merger and control cases, will be a major threat to the viability of the small carrier.

Will the rail industry react in a sensible fashion? To do so, it must recognize the transparent benefits of short-run traffic gains. For the long run, the industry still must come to grips with its inadequate return on investment and its inability to generate enough cash to replace the plant it is consuming.

But with every risk, there is opportunity. The smaller carriers will have within their grasp the ability for quicker reaction to market change. In many cases, if management does its homework, they should be able to blunt such competitive pressures and even capitalize on them.

Deregulation will certainly provide opportunities to overcome the shortfall in earnings and cash, but I do not conceive it to be a panacea. Congress, for example, has been unable so far to solve the northeast rail problem, and I suggest that this legislation will not be the answer here either. Our common carrier system instead needs significant improvements in productivity both in capital utilization and manpower. Deregulation gives us the opportunity to begin but much—in fact, much more—must come from within.

While the future is secure for the high density main lines, there remains a significant need for rationalizing the subsidiary light density lines of all railroads. Deregulation provides for quicker action in withdrawing service on such branch lines, while the provisions for retaining such service (at the expense of others) will soon instruct any supporter or purchaser of light density lines the meaning of capitalism in its purest sense. The ultimate result will be the pruning of a significant number of dead and dying limbs from the rail system. Whether through the support of shippers or government, the benefit will be in needed cost reductions.

UNWITTING ASSIST TO TRUCKERS

The rail industry must not practice internecine rate warfare. I am not alluding here to the attraction of traffic through better marketing strategies. Rather, I am speaking of selective attacks on specific segments of traffic through reducing rates below normal profit levels, producing non-remunerative "benefits" in return for the diversion of traffic or accessory charges. If such practices prevail, there will be significant reduction in the strength of our network. There will also be significant opportunities made available to the motor carrier industry to grow at the railroads' expense.

Rate fluctuations as a result of deregulation are usually construed as generally upward and often visualize long-term contracts or other methods to secure shipper obligation. As this tendency is fulfilled (and it must occur), there will be significant changes in traffic mix and, perhaps, even some dislocation of industry.

The substance of the Deregulation Act is the belief that price and service competition will provide a balance, allowing shippers and receivers a choice both among modes and carriers. Accordingly, rail sales and service efforts will most certainly evolve to reflect not only the basic transit movement but other factors, such as time allowed for all parties or specifics of equipment. These will be identified and become part of the transportation package, not unlike a model of automobile with or without the various fringes and options.

CALL FOR "TRUE" INTERMODALISM

Now here are some of the ways we might best meet the challenge of the next decade in order to survive and grow:

Intermodalism has become a trite word. Many visualize only trailers on flatcars, but it is truly much more. It is the concept of the movement of goods by two or more modes. Tank cars of sweeteners, for example, transferred and delivered to bakeries by the tank truck load. Or raw plastic moved in covered hoppers to a terminal for delivery by truck, as required by the manufacturer.

Finished automobiles, coiled steel, trailers, and containers are all part of Grand Trunk's and other railroads' intermodal marketing effort. Definitely, intermodal is a growth area of the railroad industry.

It is about time we made the transportation of freight between modes truly intermodal. It is essential that we provide total transportation. That means not a total rail system, not a total transportation capability, but *total transportation*. The use of agents, for example, to provide portions of traffic movements is perhaps a shortsighted practice as well as one leaving us vulnerable to more effective competition from other modes. Rather, the need is to move carload and truckload freight from origin to destination under one bill of lading with a given service level competitively priced.

Different price levels may well evolve for different services. Though the cost of a luxury car is far greater than that of a mini car, the end results are the same: You get from here to there. The difference is that there are many conveniences demanded in return for the higher cost of the luxury car. Likewise, rail transportation should offer various services at varying prices.

Productivity is perhaps the most challenging opportunity that exists today. Productivity is often thought of only in terms of labor, but there are many facets to this word. Though Webster defines productivity thusly—to produce goods or services having exchange value—we must think in terms of improved productivity in every aspect of our enterprise.

OPPORTUNITY VS. EFFICIENCY

Our industry cannot continue to remain competitive—and remain within the free enterprise area of our society—unless we continue to improve productivity. In our business, the ultimate measure is net-ton-miles per dollar of expense. Since over 50 percent of our revenue goes to pay wages and fringe benefits, we cannot expect to continue in operation without the productive involvement of our employees. Accordingly, a reduction in wages paid should not be required if we increase net-ton-miles or if we work smart (not harder). We must and should share the benefits of increased productivity with labor.

We cannot continue to consume facilities without generating the capability to replenish. Specifically, we cannot compete with other modes in today's climate of deregulation unless we handle more traffic at less expense, thus generating the necessary funds to renew and improve our plant.

Over the past years, rail management has, for whatever reason, contracted away opportunities for improved efficiency. Recovering managerial flexibility will require complete awareness of the need and path for survival, mutual understanding, and respect. The current agreements that restrict our ability to renew our plant must be replaced by contracts that have the twin goals of corporate existence and employee remuneration and security.

Both railroad management and labor have somehow assumed over the years the erroneous idea that railroads will never cease operation. In the past, the actions of the ICC and Congress have reinforced such beliefs, but times are changing. Many railroaders are now out of work, while others have temporary security that is fast running out. Moreover, our government is becoming increasingly reluctant to continue to support non-profit railroad operations. And the taxpayer is telling our elected officials on each new voting day that the government is reaching close to the bottom of his pocket for tax dollars that are being dispensed without responsibility.

Increased railroad employment can only come from increased business levels. To perpetuate the status quo, on the other hand, will mean reduced employment. During the decade of the '60s, employment declined 30 percent; during the '70s, an additional 17 percent. No one can thus conclude that the policies under which these reductions have taken place will now somehow strengthen our industry while enhancing job security.

To encourage progress, we must share the benefits of increased productivity with labor. In return for the sharply increased net income which productivity will most certainly bring, a portion of the resultant profits must be shared with employees at all company levels. Profit-sharing and other areas of labor-management cooperation will promote joint recognition of profit-oriented goals, including the completion of specific tasks accomplished by increased labor effort.

The need to reduce labor cost as a percentage of the total cost of railroading is important. Our revenue, restricted by our competition—much directly subsidized by the government—is further restricted by the Deregulation Act. Costs in certain areas, especially fuel and technology, are increasing at rates exceeding inflation. But labor still demands an appropriate wage, a respectable working environment, job stabilization, and security. And management must, working with labor, find the solution.

This is a difficult challenge for both sides, and there are many new faces on the scene. Their owners must focus on this issue, and I have faith that, with indications of increased understanding over the last year, a satisfactory resolution will evolve and a firm base be constructed upon which to build a stronger rail system.

BETTER UTILIZATION INVOLVES ALL

Better equipment utilization must be another byword of the need for productivity gains in the '80s. Equipment costs now average $55,000 per year. Such investment demands a rate of return of approximately $5,000 per year to equal an investment in secure Treasury bills. A daily cost of almost $14, to which must be added repairs, control, and idle days, requires maximum attention to the utilization task from the railroad (and remember a railroad is only people, labor, and management) as well as from the shippers and receivers.

Efficiency in car management is a critical need. The railroads have a smaller car fleet that they did in the '50s and '60s, but its capacity is higher and its cost of acquisition and retention is proportionally much greater. Accordingly, the highest potential for productivity improvement, next to labor, is in utilization of the car fleet and minimization of car inventory. As an industry, we have not moved aggressively or positively in this direction.

In the '60s, the railroads pioneered (and paid the price) with a car identification system. We on the GTW proved the reflector label system was cost-effective regardless of whatever other deficiencies existed. The concept and technology, however, is now widely accepted and used by other industries since the railroad industry could not support a system that was utilized by only a few of its members. No one, apparently, has expressed the thought that the industry needs the ability to be informed when a freight car is moved. I predict, however, that within three years the industry will again be considering the concept of identifying moving equipment and to automatically transmit such information to users and to computer memories.

DEVELOP TRAIN-MAKEUP SIMULATOR

Systems are being developed and tested that are utilizing today's miraculous technology and will provide reliability and inexpensive application. Tremendous improvement in our operation can result if the industry capitalizes on the opportunity.

Productivity, for example, will improve through the use of simulators and the predictive capacity of today's computers. On GTW, we are most enthusiastic about a train-makeup simulator as part of a larger computerized simulation model that we developed jointly with Stanford Research Institute.

The simulator uses computer-generated information in concert with a projected 16-hour operating plan to predict yard inventories along with train movements and makeup. The operating plan consists of instructions for each of the many trains GTW operates, including departure time, assigned horsepower, consist, route, etc.

The simulation is run at the beginning of each shift and evaluation of the reports usually leads to a modified operating plan within the first hour. Main benefit of this system: immediate accessibility to information for real-time decision-making by dispatchers and trainmasters, with an 85 percent accuracy in operating forecasts. Couple this with improved car identification and automatic dispatching, and we give our operating people valuable tools to improve responsiveness, reliability, and efficiency.

MANY CONTRIBUTE TO IMPROVED SAFETY

Although substantial progress has been made in recent years in the whole area of safety, it is a never-ending challenge and a goal that must be foremost in all rail managers' and employees' minds. Based upon experience, our forefathers established the first requirement in every operating rule book: "Safety is of the first importance in the discharge of duty." To refuse to learn from their experience will condemn us to reliving the past.

Serious personnel injuries have been reduced over the last decade. Many factors contributed—better education, improved equipment and safety devices, i.e., yard lighting, radios, etc. But there are still far too many unnecessary or preventable injuries to our employees. Increased, not reduced, attention to this basic element of railroading is mandatory.

Fostered by the 1973 Federal Highway Act that provided the first of almost $800 million for improved grade crossing protection and emphasized through education and programs such as "Operation Lifesavers," highway-rail crossing accidents have been reduced approximately one less death per million-train-miles even though automobile travel has increased 40 percent in the same period. We have made substantial progress, but much more needs to be done. We cannot lose the momentum or allow the federal and state governments' attention diverted from their responsibility. We must keep up the education program so that the motorist is always aware of the hazards.

Fortunately, the industry has been able to increase its maintenance expenditures over the last five years. Led by the large infusion of funds for Contrail's rehabilitation, almost every carrier has contributed to make our entire rail network stronger, more stable, and thus safer.

I am personally convinced that a well-maintained track structure is a primary requirement for profitability. Good track results in efficiencies and economies not readily apparent, be it reduction in crew time or reduced locomotive and car maintenance. We must continue to improve our fixed facilities. Our maintenance forces have the know-how; we as managers must give them the people, tools, and materials.

Brief mention of hazardous material transportation is in order. The rails have enabled the manufacturers of these materials to produce them more economically and more safely. We have provided transportation networks that allow distribution of the product to where it is consumed rather than requiring production at the point of consumption. I am convinced that overall, this is the safest course. The burden is upon the rail industry to carry these commodities safely. However, there is an obligation upon regulatory bodies, manufacturers, consumers, and the rail industry to address the problems of reasonable care and safety, balanced by the costs of prevention and liability.

In summary, the Challenge of the '80s is relatively straightforward: We need a national transportation policy that balances the capabilities and public need of each form of transportation. Of paramount need also is a Federal Railroad Administration that goes beyond regulations and both supports the rail industry and leads the effort for equal treatment by government.

There must be improved productivity; we must move more freight. We *have* surplus capacity, and we are the most economical and fuel-efficient mode for transporting goods over long distances. Increasing productivity results from better utilization of assets, both capital and labor.

We must continue to address the entire safety spectrum. We have made progress, but there is much to be done. The sociological climate of today's and tomorrow's society will demand improvement. Failure to take the initiative and effectively demonstrate progress will result in further loss of management control, burdensome legislation, and additional regulation.

These issues, although not new, are urgent and must effectively be addressed in the era of the 1980s. Since they are becoming more complex, they will demand more attention than in the past. It is imperative, nonetheless, that the industry meet these challenges without sacrificing the need to generate increased funds for capital and earnings growth.

© *Progressive Railroading, January 1981 (reprinted with permission)*

APPENDIX 2

SHARED VALUES

THE BURDAKIN FAMILY

JOHN HOWARD BURDAKIN, OUR FATHER, AND OUR MOTHER, JEAN Moulton Burdakin, were happily married for sixty-three years, during which they moved sixteen times as he advanced in his railroad career.

During all those moves, Dad would find a house for Mom and us, his three sons, always in an excellent school district. While our dad was running railroads, our mom became an expert in dealing with movers, making friends, and managing a household of active boys. Our parents finally settled in Bloomfield Hills, Michigan, outside of Detroit, when Dad went to work for the Grand Trunk Western Railroad.

After Dad retired from Grand Trunk, he and Mom remained in Michigan, wintering in Florida, until they moved to Colorado to be near their oldest son, John Jr., and his wife, Cynthia. Mom died of pancreatic cancer on March 30, 2012, and Dad died on September 11, 2014, in Cedar Rapids, Iowa. He'd moved there to be near his grandson Michael Burdakin and his granddaughter Julia Privett. Julia and her husband, Brian, had a son, Evan, born in 2013, our father's first great-grandchild.

Those are the facts of our parents' lives. The fabric of their lives is, of course, far richer, shot through with threads of railroad lore and family love. There was the time, for instance, when Dad took his three sons to a golf driving range, recalls son Dave, a businessman in Chicago. "Walking to the tees, we walked by a trailer, in which the owners, a couple, were arguing, using a lot of words that weren't allowed in our house," Dave says. "Dad stopped, rapped his golf club on the trailer door and shouted, 'I've got my family out here, clean up your language!' We were wide-eyed that Dad would confront them for this, risking a fight. Fortunately, it worked."

That rap on the trailer door confirmed for us that our dad was a take-charge guy. And, no doubt about it, Dad also had a cool job.

"As a little kid growing up, I thought my dad had the best job in the world, working for the Pennsylvania Railroad," says John Jr., a medical doctor in Cedar Rapids, Iowa. "Train trips were exciting adventures—going across the Isthmus of Panama on the Panama Railroad or taking a ride in the engine or the caboose, meeting railroad men and listening to some fascinating stories. I've noticed over the years that all railroad men and women, no matter in what capacity they have worked, have a love for trains that is hard to describe, but gives them a sense of community and connection."

Youngest son Dan, an Atlanta-based leader in the hospitality industry, recalls with great delight the Santa Train that his father and Art Fettig started for Grand Trunk Western employees. As an adult businessman, he now understands how the holiday Santa Trains demonstrated his dad's collaborative and caring leadership style. But as a kid, he simply knew how much fun it was to climb aboard decorated cars pulled by a diesel engine and wish people "Merry Christmas" at various Grand Trunk depots.

"Once we arrived, we would be greeted by hundreds and hundreds of smiling employees with their families, and they would walk through the train on their way to collecting gifts that we would hand them as they visited with Santa and then shook hands and conversed briefly with Mom and

Dad and other Grand Trunk executives and their families," Dan recalls. "I remember traveling to Pontiac, Royal Oak, Battle Creek, Port Huron, etc., and visiting with railroad workers who would do just about anything for my dad. They would tell me how happy they were that he was their leader, and I would know what they meant because I have been so lucky and proud to have had him as my dad and our family leader as well."

In short, we had parents who loved each other, and us, and who were partners in making sure we were well-grounded in their shared values of family, faith, integrity, service, and education.

One of the more interesting chapters in our family's many moves came in the fifteen months Dad spent as head of the Panama Railroad in 1960 to 1961. John Jr. was in second grade, David had just turned five, and Dan was one. Our mom's mother was in Massachusetts, ill with terminal pancreatic cancer. Mom somehow arranged it all, and we sailed out of New York City for the six-day trip to Panama, only to arrive and find all our household goods had been shipped to the wrong side of the canal.

Mom recalled how we boys were quite put off by the small garden lizards that cast shadows against our bedroom window shades in our Canal Zone house. Those shadows looked like monsters to us! But we became "quite blasé," she said, in sharing the silverware drawer with cockroaches and in dealing with the pervasive no-see-ums buzzing around our heads and with the occasional tarantula in a bunch of bananas. She also told a lovely story about the day she learned her mother had died, and how our housekeeper, Ermine, went about her work that day, quietly singing hymns as a source of comfort.

A highlight of our time in Panama was a ride through the canal on a banana boat, though Mom decided toddler Dan was too young for such an adventure. He stayed at our house, guarded by Ermine, who stayed awake all night, baseball bat in hand, making sure Dan was safe.

Dad, as head of the railroad, was invited to many elegant functions, and, we learned later, had to deal with some "Yankee, Go Home" unrest. Mom and Dad both welcomed chances to socialize with Panamanians and received a complimentary letter and an orchid corsage from the governor of the Canal Zone when we left the Isthmus. Our mom, in fact, sought out chances to speak Spanish with the maids at the playground where she'd take Dan, saying she'd rather do that than play bridge with the other wives.

Dad said he, too, learned a lesson during his time with the railroad there. At year's end, he'd brought in the Panama Railroad operations $8,000 under budget—only to have his boss chide him about not spending that available money! It was, he said, a major lesson in tactical government budgeting.

We were proud of both our parents, with only the normal embarrassment when our dad would be a newsmaker in his role as president of the Grand Trunk Western Railroad. John Jr., right after he'd finished ninth grade, recalls being at work with our dad one Saturday morning when our dad's assistant told him, "Your father is the best railroad man I have ever met."

"I remember these words like they were yesterday," John Jr. says. "No one had made a point of telling me this before. I was pleased to see how much respect everyone had for Dad, and I was proud to be his son. Since then, I have made it a point to do the same for other people when I meet their children, imparting positive words about their parent. I will probably never know if they will remember it, but I have a sense that it does make a difference."

It was our pleasure to see our parents have so many years together in a comfortable retirement—though we know it took Dad a few years to get over not going into the office every weekday, plus Saturday mornings.

And though this book is about Dad, it cannot be overemphasized how Mom's love and support allowed him to focus his energies on his job. She was a rock for the whole family. In a collection of stories she wrote about her life, she explained the origins of her renowned patience:

"The most hurtful thing ever spoken to me was on a visit back to my hometown after the stillborn, full-term loss of our first baby. 'Well, Jean, perhaps it is just as well. You really don't have the patience it takes to be a mother.' Those words were spoken by one of my closest high school friends. I shook for more than an hour from the horror of those words. I finally recovered enough from the crushing blow to think on the words that had been spoken. Perhaps they were true. I solemnly vowed to myself that day that if patience had been my weakness, from that day on, it would be my strength. My shoulders stopped sagging. What a gift I had been given. 'Patience will be my strength.'"

Mom admitted she was, by nature, still impatient with situations, but not with people, though she had to work at it. "Whenever in the raising of three sons, my patience was sorely tested, I remembered that patience was in the palm of my hand, and I didn't let it go. The cruel words had given me the power to will myself to be a better person. My husband and sons all benefited."

Dad often remarked that our mom never complained. He also was proud of her finesse in social situations. She didn't have much to do directly with the railroads he worked for, but she did step in one night to welcome guests to a Grand Trunk traffic dinner in Milwaukee when Dad's plane had been delayed in Philadelphia. She was on his arm at many social occasions and on trips, meeting and conversing with Canadian prime ministers and railroad conductors with equal grace. She also dealt with many of the French-Canadian spouses of Canadian National executives who would speak French at the wives' get-togethers, knowing she was an English speaker but not realizing she also understood everything they were saying in French.

Our mom had an innate stillness about her that allowed her to listen, ask appropriate questions, and get people to open up. Our dad would shake his head in amazement, remembering occasions like the company dinner in Newfoundland when a leading businessman told Mom the details of his recent divorce and asked her advice.

Our dad said many times of his "Jeannie" that "I could not have found a better, more sympathetic wife." To which we three can only add: We could not have found better parents.

In his retirement, Dad played a lot of golf at the Bloomfield Hills Country Club. He had a handicap of between thirteen and fifteen and won one senior division championship in a club tournament. Dad also was an excellent woodworker, bringing the same sense of perfection to that craft as he did to the executive suite, creating an heirloom dollhouse and rocking horse for his grandchildren. Dad also volunteered about fifteen years at the William Beaumont Hospital in Birmingham, Michigan. He would say, when pushing wheelchairs at the hospital, that he had retired from the railroad but was still in transportation. "And just like when I was working, they don't move unless I push."

Dad and Mom also spent around twenty winters at their condo in Naples, Florida, where Dad was put in charge of the condo association's books and, of course, discovered rules weren't being followed and that association members were paying too much in fees. He slyly admits that bit of news made him "a hero" to his fellow condo owners, even though we could have predicted that outcome.

During those winters in Florida, Mom cotaught memoir writing workshops. She and Dad taught English to Spanish-speaking immigrants, though Dad says he wasn't very good at that. They remained active in their church and attentive to each other's needs.

On behalf of our family, we would like to thank our parents for their steadfast example of how to live an honorable life. We'd like to thank Dennis J. Gilstad for envisioning and sponsoring this book, and Gary M. Andrew for coordinating its publication. We would like to thank Art Fettig for his work on Grand Trunk safety programs and for the recollections he wrote and shared with us about Dad and the "good track" Grand Trunk.

We would like to close this chapter with one of our mom's poems, "Insight," believing our dad when he advised young people to choose carefully whom they marry because 90 percent of their happiness—or unhappiness—would result from that decision.

> When you awaken in the night
> Don't toss and turn, wrestling with problems
> That are not yours to solve.
> Turn things over to God, and know that
> In His good time, problems will be resolved,
> Piece by piece by piece.
> Ah, sweet sleep, awake refreshed, not exhausted!

Jean and John Burdakin, 1989. (Photo from John H. Burdakin collection)

JEAN BURDAKIN ESSAYS

Following are excerpts from Jean Burdakin's "My Life: Stories for My Children," a collection of essays she wrote late in life. Jean, a graduate of Radcliffe College, married John Burdakin in 1948. She focused on her family and excelled in the role of mother to their three sons and wife of a fast-tracked executive. She managed sixteen moves before she and John settled in Bloomfield Hills, Michigan, when he began his career at Grand Trunk Western Railroad.

MY WORLD WAR II YEARS

Encouraged by my parents, I expected to attend the Bridgewater Normal School to train to be a teacher. Several of my high school friends had been accepted at Radcliffe. Early in the summer, I decided that I, too, would rather commute to Radcliffe in Cambridge than live at Bridgewater.

I phoned and made an appointment with the Dean of Admissions, Mrs. Elliott. She suggested that I take the College Board exams in August, adding that there were still two openings in the freshman class. I did this and was elated the day my acceptance arrived in the mail.

That summer, four other high school friends and I delivered gas bills, temporarily replacing men who had gone into the service. People moved around without fear in those days. Certainly the summer was a healthy one, with us walking an average of about ten miles each working day.

Between my freshman and sophomore years, I helped care for two little children on Martha's Vineyard for a month. I spent the rest of the summer working at the Walter Baker Chocolate Mill, helping make D rations—high-energy, high-nutrition chocolate bars that didn't melt in the hot temperatures of the South Pacific where our troops might need them. Have you ever smelled like a chocolate bar? My family was quick to tell me that I did! The people sitting beside me on the bus rides to East Milton on my way home may actually have enjoyed the aroma. They never said.

Between my sophomore and junior years, I spent the summer with two Radcliffe friends at Ferncroft Inn in Wonalancet, New Hampshire. We waited on tables in the dining room of this lovely inn where very genteel, mostly older, guests spent much of the summer. We each served the same table, three meals a day, all summer. We became very well-acquainted with the guests at our table. I was very lucky. Mrs. Pickering, an active member of the Boston American Association of University Women, saw to it that I was given an AAUW scholarship.

Several of us stayed on an extra couple of weeks and so were still there when the exciting news came August 14, 1945, of the surrender of Japan. The blond maintenance man promptly grabbed a bottle of vodka or rye and drank it as he hooted and hollered, driving the inn's tractor around and around the field.

As in high school, my favorite outside activity in college was singing, this time with the Radcliffe Choral Society under the direction of G. Wallace Woodworth, known affectionately as "Woody."

A special memory are the evenings we presented a Christmas program with the Harvard Glee Club in Appleton Chapel in Harvard Yard. Another is when a group of us traveled to sing a Sunday concert with the Yale Glee Club at a church in New Haven. Word came that Saturday afternoon that President Roosevelt had died. That evening, Yale's famed Whiffenpoofs male chorus stood under our window and serenaded us.

On May 7, 1945, during my sophomore year, we sang with the Boston Symphony Orchestra under the direction of the brilliant conductor Serge Koussevitzky. We were to sing the "Ode to Joy" in English—typically, it's sung in German, but we were at war with Germany—but the conductor was late coming to the podium. The orchestra members, the choral group, and the audience stirred, wondering where he was.

Suddenly, the strikingly handsome, gray-haired conductor strode onto the stage, flung off his black cape, and declared, "Ladies and gentlemen, the 'var vith' Germany is over!"

He led the orchestra in "The Star-Spangled Banner," sung by all, with tears flowing freely down most faces. We then sang Beethoven's dramatic "Ode to Joy" with hearts bursting. My parents, sitting at home listening on the radio, told me the radio announcer said the "Ode to Joy" surely had never been sung like that before and probably never would be again.

Remembering that evening when emotions soared out of sight makes me think of a very different evening during the war.

A few of us from the Choral Society were selected to sing aboard the USS *Wasp*, an aircraft carrier, on Christmas Eve 1944. The first *Wasp* had been sunk in the South Pacific. We were overwhelmed by the size of the ship.

Our singing of Christmas music was at the end of the evening program. We finished with "Silent Night," with all the sailors joining with us. As far as we could see in that enormous area of the ship, on every level, were sailors. As their voices so quietly, so beautifully, so reverently joined ours, there was an awareness of the absolute beauty of this moment in time and an acute sense of the preciousness of it. What lay ahead for these men and this ship, none of us knew.

MY CELLAR MAY BE YOUR BASEMENT

For all of my growing-up years in East Milton, Massachusetts, the cellar was the below-ground portion of the house. The only time I heard the word "basement" used was at school, the below-ground area where the lavatories were.

In those days in Boston and environs, young students would never think of raising their hands to ask, "May I please go to the bathroom?" The question always was, "May I please go to the basement?" Of course, the teacher of the first grade class usually had the good sense to say "yes." One day, Miss Cole didn't. I am sure she wishes she had. Actually, I wish she had, too. In future years, whenever I saw the boy who was the victim of the word "no," I remembered those first grade days and those moments of his misery and humiliation. I have no memory of Miss Cole saying "no" again.

Years later, John and I moved to Coshocton, Ohio, in the late fall of 1948. During one of our early visits to the home of new friends, someone mentioned bringing something up from the basement. The ensuing conversation revealed that for them the cellar was a place for storing vegetables, canned goods, seedlings, etc. The basement was the below-ground level of their houses.

Before that evening was over, I had one other learning experience. Someone mentioned that the "crick" was high. At first I was confused. Then I smiled with delight, saying, "Oh, you mean the 'creek.'" "No," the man replied, "I mean the 'crick.'" Properly put in my place, from that moment on, as I moved from state to state, I tried to discipline myself never to say, "Oh, you mean."

I did slip up once in about 1965 when we moved to Pittsburgh. My very dear neighbor and friend, Pat Mansmann, mentioned the "tarr." At first, I drew a total blank as to what she was saying. Then inspiration struck. I declared eagerly, "Oh, you mean 'tower.'" I heard myself this time. I quickly assured her that "tarr" sounded equally as good as "tower" any day of the week and confessed my weakness for using the unfortunate phrase, "Oh, you mean," as I traveled about. Whew! A *new* resolution—the *same* resolution!

HOUSE HUNTING

In our moves around the United States, John, the pragmatic one, made sure there would be room in the house for the five of us, while I noted which house had the prettiest yard.

When we were house hunting in Pittsburgh, John thought one house with a very lovely yard was a bit small but was willing to consider it. The real estate agent, having first phoned that we were coming, let us in. The lady of the house was seated on the sofa, painting her nails bright red. A son in his late twenties, sitting in a chair, smoked as he stared at us. The French poodle was friendly as we apologetically passed through the room—noting that the beige, wall-to-wall carpet was a virtual sea of small yellow stains.

Exploring the house included a trip to the lower level. We passed through the washer-dryer area and into a long, narrow family room with small windows on the right side and at the end. John, the engineer, thought to himself—why on earth do they have a closed drape on the middle of the inside wall?

To satisfy his curiosity, he pulled on the gizmo that opened the drapes. Immediately, he found himself at very close range with a life-size photographic enlargement of the nude, well-endowed upper body of the lady sitting on the sofa upstairs. The three of us laughed till the tears ran. Then we realized we had a problem. How were we going to pass back through the living room with our faces straight? We finally mustered enough self-control for a *fast* exit.

The house we actually bought had its own set of peculiarities. We detected a few problems as we looked at it. However, it seemed fresh and clean. There was plenty of room for all of us and a beautiful view.

Well, no wonder the house looked fresh and clean. When we arrived on moving-in day, we immediately discovered that the lady of *this* house had taken a large roller and painted *around* the furniture—in every room of the house!

I WOULD HAVE MISSED ALL THIS, IF I HAD SAID "NO!"

Carrol Falberg, my yoga instructor and good friend, asked me to fill in at the last minute as co-captain of the 1993 home tour in Birmingham, Michigan.

I said "yes," and on Monday morning, Carrol and I went to "our house" for a preview tour.

The decorator opened the door and welcomed us. He introduced us to the very lovely young lady of the house, to her toddler son, and to her two-week-old baby son. We had noticed the plumbing truck outside. The plumber was upstairs fixing a leak. A nanny was helping with the boys. Many beautiful floral arrangements had been delivered. Two furniture movers were carrying a large armoire up the narrow stairs and scratched the paint, necessitating a quick repair. The phone kept ringing, and the pest control people were in the kitchen trying to catch five baby squirrels that had gotten into the kitchen through a panel in a cabinet. Three mice had found their way in on Sunday, the day before.

By the time we had finished our preview tour, five squirrels had been live-trapped. Two more were running around. As the pest control man tried to put two baby squirrels in a box, one in each hand, we watched transfixed as, unknown to the man, a third baby squirrel ran up his pant leg, across his back, and around the man, as the second pest control man grabbed it. About then, I finally closed my mouth—which was gaping wide!

Was I ever so young that I could handle all that confusion in my home with at least surface calmness and a pleasant smile?! I wonder. The young woman who owned the home certainly did!

The next day, during the home tour, I was assigned to the kitchen by the back door and tour exit. I stood there imagining the scene if the squirrels had suddenly put in their appearance on Tuesday instead of Monday—or, for that matter, the mice! Would I have risen to the occasion with unflappable dignity—or would I have been the first one out the back door?

APPENDIX 4

THIS I BELIEVE

JOHN BURDAKIN DELIVERED THIS SPEECH AT A MARCH 24, 1981, luncheon at Fort Street Presbyterian Church in Detroit. It was one in a series of speeches delivered by community leaders on their personal belief systems. These thoughts seem an appropriate way to end a book about a man who attempted to live his personal and professional life by the highest standards.

"This I Believe"—what a challenging subject. When one considers that "what I believe" is the very foundation and continuing criteria by which one individual lives his or her life, it is a profound subject. One cannot expect justice to be done in the limited time allotted. Yes, en route to fellowship and lunch, it is your lot to be subjected to my attempt to briefly address this subject.

I accepted this gracious invitation to chat with you today for two reasons. Foremost was the pleasant association I had worshipping in this magnificent church in 1970 while waiting for my family to follow my transfer to Detroit. Mr. Crilley has done a superb job of blending the heritage of this congregation with the needs of today. Fort Street continues to be a valuable and vital part of the Detroit scene and deserves the support of all of us.

The other reason I felt compelled to respond to the honor of the invitation was the challenge it presented. My career has been very demanding. The railroad industry never allows the wheels to stand still—movement occurs every hour of every day, and so an operations manager never truly has the opportunity to divorce himself and reflect on his personal life and his role within this world. Thus, it has been a challenge to focus on a constructive message for today.

Further, to present my personal thoughts and philosophy to you—in fact, to anyone—is a new experience. I have generally relied more upon example than teaching. The more I endeavored to crystallize my thinking, the more I realized that to present "This I Believe" to you in a meaningful and thought-stimulating manner would be a fascinating challenge.

My education was engineering and thus my mind is conditioned to rationalize and decide based upon proven theorems. Every developing human being endeavors to sort out and establish the foundation upon which he will build his or her life. Each of us, at some point, has to ask, why am I here? Where am I going? Where do I want to go? How do I get there? And, again, why am I here?

Now, I don't know if an engineer wrestles with these questions in a different manner, but I am sure we each, some more deeply and thoroughly than others, are confronted with these concerns as we develop and proceed through life. Underlying these questions, as fundamental and encompassing as they may be, is the subject of this series. "This I Believe" is the foundation from which we direct our paths through this world.

Before I address the first question I raised, "Why am I here?," there is a larger, more fundamental question that I do not even try to answer. This is: "Why is there life and people on this world?" What is the master plan of the Earth, and does it fit into a larger system as our heart fits into and serves our body?

I have never had any insight into a potential answer to this—or even a path to a solution. I also have decided that there may be no resolution to this problem. There certainly is no indication as to the basic reason for the world as we know it. And so I have backed away from trying to resolve this; I have been able to accept comfortably the existence of our planet. To do otherwise would consume my energies in nonproductive efforts.

Having accepted Earth and life thereon, where do I go? It becomes evident that each of us is a combination of the body we are born with, that we inherited from our parents and ancestors, and of the experiences we obtain as we progress through life.

The first of these two is not of our making. We inherit our physical, mental, and personal traits. These are given to us, and from our day of birth, our development is then a result of the events and experiences that occur to us. Each person and his entire being is the summation of the effect of his daily contacts with his portion of the world. Each contact with another being, each page we read, each sound we hear, each walk through the city or countryside—yes, each experience, big or small, impacts on the individual.

I envision each person as a building, a house, if you will, that is made up of many bricks or stones mortared together. Little experiences are little stones placed to keep the larger stones stable within the structure. Each large or small building block builds and contributes to the size, the beauty, the purpose of the individual. And we should not be critical of another's house, for we do not know of his experiences and his opportunities to build upon his inheritance.

But it does not take many of these building blocks or stones to realize there is behind this world a master guiding force. We may not understand why life is on Earth, but one cannot doubt that there is a plan for that life on Earth as exhibited by every tangible object, be it living or inert. And this plan has to be conceived, directed, and executed by an overriding force. Who can look at the forms of life, follow each through the cycle from birth to death, and not know that we are being directed by a supreme being?

If this were not so, how could the pieces fit together? The obvious example is the propagation of life, and the delicate but essential relationship between those forms of continually regenerated life. The water cycle from oceans to moisture, to clouds, to rain, to Earth, to support life and return to the oceans. The interdependent food cycle that may seem harsh—such as worms to nourish fowl, to nourish man. There are so many examples—can anyone truly believe God is not there? Even the primitive people worshipped a supreme power. We have the benefit of the written account of both the Old and New Testaments.

Now, I am not a student of the Bible. In fact, I have never taken the time to read the Good Book through from cover to cover. Just what is the purpose of the Bible? Why has it succeeded in affecting the lives of almost every human being on Earth, either directly or indirectly? Obviously, it is far more than a historical account. Is it not a part of the Lord's plan?

In my simple, uninformed rationalization, let me suggest the two main purposes that are addressed by the Bible. The first is the rules, the examples, and the leadership to guide and encourage us to improve this Earth through our lives. The second is to provide support for us as we meet our personal burdens.

Included in the latter area is the forgiveness necessary to permit our accepting our failure to meet His standards or to accomplish our personally set goals. When we feel inadequate, we must recover our self-respect, our direction, and our determination to again move forward. Few can get it all together without outside assistance. The greatest source for this support, essential for continued constructive and contributing life, comes from the teachings of the Bible. Who is there who can read or hear the Twenty-Third Psalm and not be fortified to face the future?

I am a believer in the setting of goals. It is impossible to know or realize change unless we mark the starting place. It is likewise impossible to record progress unless we set mileposts along the way. But the setting of goals is a complex subject in itself and one I will not address here. Suffice it to say, we all need to set goals, goals that are achievable yet challenging. But goals have a definite bearing on the questions of why—why?—why?—that I asked earlier.

In rationalizing the why—"Why am I here?"—I come to one basic thought. From this base, my individual goals, both short-term and long-term, have been placed and by experience supported. Thus, the primary "This I Believe," the underlying support for my life, resolves down to the answer of "why I'm here." I can only define the answer as "to improve this Earth." Obviously, I do not have the power to stop "man's inhumanity to man," but I do have the power to give someone support when needed, a challenge for his life, make and assure a safer environment, give of myself to improve the status of my fellow man.

If each of us contributed even a slight effort every day toward this end, the cumulative effect is beyond the power of imagination. The alternative is very vivid, clear, and disastrous.

This basic creed—"to leave this world in a better condition than when I arrived"—has given me great comfort and support in meeting the challenges I've faced, in arriving at the decisions I've had to make, in maintaining the determination necessary to bring those decisions to fruition.

This philosophy has inspired my goals. Each task set has been and is carried out under this creed. Each day is one more building stone of my house. Each experience has bearing upon the characteristics that were inherited upon birth and, with this fundamental target, those experiences have permitted development toward the ultimate.

This I believe—to live my life so that the Earth will be a better place for my having passed through.

Notes

INTRODUCTION

1. Mary Sharp conducted interviews with John Burdakin from January to September 2014 in Cedar Rapids, Iowa. Anecdotes in this book also come from tape recordings Burdakin made with family members and with Gary M. Andrew in Colorado Springs, Colorado, in 2013.

2. The Interstate Commerce Commission (icc) was established in 1887 with the responsibility of regulating all railroads engaged in interstate commerce. It had purview over the reasonableness of railroad rates and service, the limits to operating territories, and the ability to exit from markets. The icc's charge was significantly altered in 1980 with the Staggers Act. The icc was eventually replaced by the Surface Transportation Board in 1995.

3. Donald V. Harper, *Transportation in America* (Englewood Cliffs, NJ: Prentice-Hall, 1982), 497–98.

4. Ibid., 518–21.

5. "Brief History of Consolidated Rail Corporation," Www.conrail.com/history.

6. The National Railway Passenger Corporation (nrpc) was formed in 1970 and designed to take over operation of rail passenger service in the contiguous forty-eight states. Railroads were encouraged to become shareholders in the

NRPC by either investing cash or rolling stock. Participating railroads would be able to discontinue rail passenger service as of May 1, 1971. A total of twenty railroads agreed to participate to what became known as Amtrak which ran its first train in May 1971. Rather than become stockholders, sixteen of the participating carriers applied their contribution to their federal income taxes. See Harper, *Transportation in America*, 382–86.

7. "The 1900s, Railroads in the 20th Century," American-Rails.com.

8. Rail shipments traveled along a specific route that was associated with a particular rate. Routes could contain any number of carriers that had agreed how to divide the revenue from the shipment. For example, a shipment from Philadelphia to Chicago could be routed PRR or alternatively PRR-Detroit-GTW. Shippers had the power to specify the route to be used. If it wasn't specified, then the originating carrier could select whatever route it preferred. As a rule, originating carriers would always try to maximize their longest haul. Smaller carriers, such as the Grand Trunk Western, needed to encourage shippers to include it in a route even though it may mean more interchanges and a longer transit time.

9. "CSX Merger Family Tree," Trains.com, June 2, 2006.

10. Crown Corporations are a Canadian invention that is a hybrid organization between a government body and a private enterprise. There is some similarity to the Amtrak and Conrail models. The CN was privatized in 1995. See Kazi Stastna, "What are Crown Corporations and Why Do They Exist?" *CBC News*, April 1, 2012.

11. See appendix 1, which includes an article, "The '80s: Now Even More Challenging," that John Burdakin prepared for *Progressive Railroading* in January 1981. In it, he discusses the many problems and opportunities brought on by a deregulated environment—many of which are highlighted in this book.

CHAPTER 1. WHEN PUT IN CHARGE, TAKE CHARGE

1. Philip Fine, "Farmer's Son Transformed CN," *Toronto Globe and Mail*, November 6, 2010.

2. Grand Trunk Corporation (GTC) was a holding company for CN's U.S. subsidiaries.

3. To get an idea of just how big that show was, see appendix 1 for the report Burdakin wrote for *Progressive Railroading* in 1981.

4. For more information, see Don L. Hofsommer, *Grand Trunk Corporation: Canadian National Railways in the United States, 1971–1992* (East Lansing: Michigan State University Press, 1995).

5. This is an example of needing Interstate Commerce Commission approval to abandon a service by going through a process.

6. Rule G prohibits the use of alcohol or drugs while on duty or expecting a call to duty. It is part of the standard code for the Association of American Railroads.

7. Art Fettig and Joe Carpenter, *The Santa Train: The Train That Nobody Seemed to Care About* (published by the author, 2014).

8. Brass bearings, or friction bearings, required lubrication at every yard stop to prevent overheating. Friction-bearing cars were not allowed in interchange service after 1980. Cars built after 1966 are required to have roller bearings that are sealed and do not need frequent lubrication.

CHAPTER 2. DO THE RIGHT THING

1. Trainmasters have broad responsibility for trains arriving, being organized, and dispatched from a specific terminal, that is, a rail yard.

2. J. K. Daughen and P. Binzen, *The Wreck of the Penn Central* (Frederick, MD: Beard Books, 1999). The Penn Central failed in June 1970.

3. The Interstate Commerce Commission (ICC) was established in 1887 with the responsibility of regulating all railroads engaged in interstate commerce. It had purview over the reasonableness of railroad rates and service, the limits to operating territories, and the ability to exit from markets. In 1968, a railroad needed permission from the ICC to abandon passenger service even though the service may have been unprofitable. The ICC's charge was significantly altered in 1980 with the Staggers Act. The ICC was eventually replaced by the National Surface Transportation Board in 1995.

4. It should be noted that even had Perlman accepted Burdakin's recommendation, he could not have voted on it. The boards of the Pennsylvania Railroad and New York Central had approved the merger, and Penn Central chairman Stuart Saunders was accepting of the merger terms.

CHAPTER 3. WHEN YOU SEE A PROBLEM, FIND SOLUTIONS

1. The concept was an extension of the intermodal concept, i.e., the combination of two modes of transportation to extract the best of each mode. Early intermodal service focused on "piggybacks," which involved a complete highway trailer, with wheels, on a flat car. The Flexi-Van concept needed a special flat car with a turntable that allowed the van to pivot in transferring it from truck to rail. Loading and unloading the van were considerably easier than loading highway trailers "circus style." The service was eventually replaced by containers lifted onto standard flat cars by cranes or portable lifts. See Tom Berg, "Just an Old Trailer? No—It's Part of Intermodal History," Truckinginfo, October 15, 2013, http://www.truckinginfo.com.
2. Art Fettig, "Always Mr. Burdakin to Me" (2013), unpublished.
3. Trackage rights is an agreement between railroads that allows one to travel over the other's right-of-way in exchange for compensation. In some cases, trackage rights could be imposed by regulatory bodies—for example, the ICC—to preserve competitive balance. They are often a condition of mergers and acquisitions. Also, they can be negotiated between railroads when there are mutual benefits.
4. Even after the Staggers Act was passed in 1980, railroads needed the ICC's permission to merge or acquire other rail properties in the interest of preserving competition.
5. Gus Welty, "The Meaning of Merger," *Railway Age*, July 1984, 73–74.
6. Don L. Hofsommer, *Grand Trunk Corporation: Canadian National Railways in the United States, 1971–1992* (East Lansing: Michigan State University Press, 1995), 115.

7. Ibid., 119. The GTW had always considered Cincinnati an important gateway once it acquired the DT&I. However, the gateway began to lose its promise when CSX merged with the Louisville and Nashville (L&N) and then the Norfolk Western and the Southern merged to form the NS.

CHAPTER 4. YOU WON'T WIN THEM ALL

1. For a brief history of the development of ACI, see Keith Thompson, "Tracking Freight Cars," *Trains*, May 6, 2006, http://trn.trains.com.
2. Ibid. The new technology is called Automatic Equipment Identification (AEI). It is a radio frequency transponder located on both sides of the car. It has an accuracy rate of 99.9 percent. The Association of American Railroads mandated that all cars and locomotives be tagged by the end of 1994.
3. Don L. Hofsommer, *Grand Trunk Corporation: Canadian National Railways in the United States, 1971–1992* (East Lansing: Michigan State University Press, 1995), 98.
4. Byron Olsen, "Milwaukee Road's Rescue Was Soo Line's Triumph," *Trains Magazine*, April 2013, 40.
5. "Grand Trunk Corporation: CN's Successful Experiment," presentation by Grand Trunk executive Howard M. Tischler to the Lexington Group, October 2, 2010, Calgary.
6. Ibid. It was estimated the CN system could put eighty thousand revenue cars a year on the Milwaukee.
7. Hofsommer, *Grand Trunk Corporation*, 104.
8. Railroad mergers can be classified as either "end-to-end" or "side-by-side." The economic promise of end-to-end mergers is that service will improve— for example, by eliminating interchanges between independent railroads or creating run-through service. The increased service should attract increased business—at least in theory. The economic promise for side-by-side mergers is to eliminate duplicate facilities and other assets, such as parallel lines. The difficulty is that these mergers always result in a loss of service to the shipping public, which the regulators are supposed to protect. In the Milwaukee case,

the c&nw was clearly a side-by-side merger where the Soo had more end-to-end characteristics.

9. Olsen, "Milwaukee Road's Rescue," 42.

CHAPTER 5. HIRE GOOD PEOPLE

1. For further understanding of just how bad things became at Penn Central, see Joseph R. Daughen and Peter Binzen, *The Wreck of the Penn Central*, 2nd ed. (Frederick, MD: Beard Books, 1999).

CHAPTER 6. CHOOSE CAREFULLY WHOM YOU MARRY

1. Jean Burdakin, "My Life: Stories for My Children," part of a writing workshop she cotaught, unpublished. See appendix 2.

CHAPTER 7. ENJOY YOUR WORK AND WORK HARD

1. Dan Burdakin, *Suite Talk: A Guide to Business Excellence* (Atlanta: Lead Goose Publishing, 2003).

Index

Page numbers in italics refer to pictures.

A

Adams, Bob, 50

Association of American Railroads, 43–44

B

Baltimore and Ohio Railroad (B&O), xvix, 41

Bandeen, Robert, xiv, 3–4, 16, 20, 26, 35; as Burdakin's mentor, 12–13, 49; and Jean Burdakin, 55–56

Battle Creek, MI, 10, 35

Blanchard, James, *18*

Brown, Warren, 7

Burdakin, Dan, 64–65, 82

Burdakin, David "Dave," 82

Burdakin, Dorothy, 60

Burdakin, Eleanor, 60–61

Burdakin, Jean, *54*, 55–56, 63, 81, 84–85, *88*

Burdakin, John H.: childhood of, 12, 58–62; communication skills of, 2, 8, 11, 15; confidence of, 13–15; corporate goals of, 11–12; family of, 64–65, 59–62, 81–87; integrity of, 24–27; labor relations of, 2, 7–10, 25, 44, 74–75; management style of, 1–7, 11–12, 15–17, 19–23, 51–52, 64; marriage of, *54*, 55–57; on the need for rules, 19–23, 30–35, 38; in Reserve Officers' Training Corps (ROTC), 13; retirement of, 26–27, 83–84, *88*; on safety, 29–35; Voluntary Coordination Agreement and, 45–46; during World War II, 13–15. *See also* Grand Trunk Western Corporation (GTC); Grand Trunk Western Railroad (GTW)

Burdakin, John H., Jr., 82, 84

Burdakin, Martha, *54*, *58*, 59, 61–62

Burdakin, Richard, *54*, *58*, 59

Burlington Northern Railway (BN), xvi, xx

C

Canadian National Railway (CN), xx, 3, 11–13, 16, 26, 36, 44–45, 55

Canadian Pacific Railway, xvi

Central Vermont Railway, xxv, 3, 44–45

Chesapeake and Ohio Railway (C&O), xvix

Chessie System, xvix
Chicago, Burlington and Quincy Railroad, xx
Chicago, Milwaukee, St. Paul and Pacific
    Railroad. *See* Milwaukee Road
Cincinnati, OH, 21–22, 30
Claypool, Ed, 51–52
Cole, Basil, 37, 50
Coleman, William T., 70
Conrail, xvii, xvix, 37, 68
Coshocton, OH, 22, 92; 1950 train wreck
    at, *28*, 29–30
Cramer, Walter H., 4
Crown Corporation, xx, 13, 102 (n. 10)
CSX, xvii, xix, 37

D

Dakota, Minnesota and Eastern Railroad, xvi
Daley, Richard, *xiv*
Delmarva Peninsula, 41
Detroit, MI, 4, 5, 7–8, 10, 35–38, 45, 50
Detroit, Toledo and Ironton Railroad
    (DT&I), xvix, 45, 50
Detroit & Toledo Shore Line Railway, 50
Dole, Elizabeth, 37
Duluth, Missabe and Iron Railroad
    (DM&IR), 35
Duluth, MN, *xxiv*, 35–36, 45
Duluth, Winnipeg & Pacific Railway
    (DWP), xxv, 3, 35–36, 45
Dunnville, Rosemary, 26
Durand, MI, *xxvi*, 5–6

E

Elliott, James, 50

F

Federal Highway Administration, 36
Federal Railroad Administration, 37–38,
    70, 78
Fettig, Art, xiv, 10, 34–35, 50–51, 82, 86
Flexi-Van, 31, 104 (n. 1)
Flint, MI, 10
Ford, Gerald, *xiv*
Fort Belvoir, Virginia, 14
Fortune magazine, 7

G

Gelease, Jimmy, 21–22
General Motors, xx
Gilstad, Dennis, 86
Glavin, Bill, 5, 50
Grand Trunk Western Corporation (GTC),
    3, 7, 12, 26, 46
Grand Trunk Western Railroad (GTW): and
    auto industry, xxi, 8; Automatic Car
    Identification, 43–44, 76; "Burdakin
    Blue," 8; computerization, 8, 76; cor-
    porate goals, 11–12; deficits, 3–4; ferry,
    33; "Good Track Road," 8, 78; hot box
    detectors, 16; impact of Staggers Act,
    xx–xxi, 70–72; impact of trucking on,
    xx, 68–69, 72; labor relations, 2, 7–12,
    15, 43; mergers, xvix–xxi, 45–46, 105
    (n. 8); "Rule G," 9, 103 (n. 6); safety,
    31–35, 77–78; Santa Train, 10–11,
    82–83; trailers on flatcars, 31; training,
    6–7; Voluntary Coordination Agree-
    ment, 45–46
Great Northern Railway, xx
GT Reporter, 11

H

Hasbrook, Doug, 29

I

intermodal service, 31, 73, 104 (n. 1)
Interstate Commerce Act of 1887, xvi
Interstate Commerce Commission (ICC),
    xvi–xix, 25, 71, 101 (n. 2), 103 (n. 3,
    chap. 2); and Grand Trunk Western
    Railroad, xvii–xviii, 36 -37, 50

J

Johnson, "Big George," 2

K

Kalamazoo, MI, 33
Kentucky Derby, 23
Kohl, Huck, 33, 35

L

Lansing, MI, 10, 33
LeClair, J. Maurice, 26–27
Litfin, William, Sr., 4–5
Louisville, KY, 23
Louisville and Nashville Railroad (L&N), xvix

M

Maas, Gerry, 26
Massachusetts Institute of Technology (MIT), xxiii, 13–16, 56, 62
McGhee, Carl, 15–16
Michigan Railroad History Museum, xiv, xv, xxvi, 6, 18, 48
Michigan State University, 33
Milwaukee Road, xvii, xx, 45
Moss, Hy, 20
Moulton, Jane, *54*
Moulton, George, *54*

N

National Guard, 29
National Railway Passenger Corporation, 101 (n. 6)
New York, New Haven and Hartford Railroad (New Haven), 25
New York Central Railroad, xvi, 31–32
Norfolk Southern Railway (NS), xvii, 37
Northern Lines Merger, xx
Northern Pacific Railway, xx

P

Panama Railroad, xxiv, 30, *66*, 83–84
Pennsylvania Railroad (Penn Central), xvi–xvii, 68–69; Burdakin experience with, 2–3, 15–17, 19–23, 25–26, 28–30, 41–43, 63–64; 1950 Coshocton wreck, 29–30

Perlman, Alfred E., 25, 30–31
Phi Kappa Sigma, 62
Pittsburgh and Lake Erie Railroad, 50
Pontiac, MI, 5, 8, 10, 36
Port Huron, MI, 5, 10
Privett, Brian, 82
Privett, Evan, *58*, 82
Privett, Julie, 82
Progressive Railroading, 79

R

Radcliffe College, 55–57, 89–90
Railroad Reorganization Acts, 69
Roeper, Park, 41

S

Santa Train, 10–11, 82–83
Seaboard Coast Line Railroad (SCL), xvix
Sheetz, George, 16
Soo Line, 46
Southeastern Michigan Transportation Authority, 36
Spokane Portland & Seattle Railway, xx
Staggers Act of 1980, xv, xviii, xvix–xx, 45, 70

T

Tischler, Howard M., 7
Toronto Globe and Mail, 3

U

Union Pacific Railroad, xvi, xx

W

William Beaumont Hospital, 85
Wooden, Donald G., 4
World War II: Jean Burdakin on, 90–91; John Burdakin's service in, 13–15, 56, *58*, 62